NKJV

SPIRIT-FILLED LIFE® BIBLE

THIRD EDITION

BY THE BOOK SERIES:
ACTS

EXECUTIVE EDITOR
Jack W. Hayford, Litt.D.

THOMAS NELSON

Since 1798

www.ThomasNelson.com

Spirit-Filled Life® Mission Statement

The mission of *Spirit-Filled Life*® Bibles and reference products is to serve the body of Christ with a broad range of trustworthy products marked by biblical soundness, balanced scholarship, and a sense of honor toward the modern-day working of the Holy Spirit. These resources are designed to provide biblical equipping for practical living in God's kingdom and around the world.

Spirit-Filled Life® *Bible,* Third Edition, Acts
Copyright © 2018 by Thomas Nelson.
Published in Nashville, Tennessee, by Thomas Nelson.
Thomas Nelson is a registered trademark of HarperCollins Christian Publishing, Inc.

The Holy Bible, New King James Version, copyright © 1982 by Thomas Nelson. All rights reserved.
Concordance copyright © 1995 by Thomas Nelson.
Project management by Thinkspot Communications, Franklin, TN

Library of Congress Control Number: 2021931464

BY THE BOOK SERIES

You are holding a single book of the Bible from the *Spirit-Filled Life®
Bible*. Even though it is only one book, it certainly does not lack content.
This robust edition, which includes interleaved journal pages, offers a
compact and portable way to study this special book of the Bible. It also
gives you a taste of what the full *Spirit-Filled Life Bible* has to offer. If
you find your study of Acts as rewarding as we expect you will, consider obtaining a copy of the full Bible to continue your studies.

Keep in mind that this book is taken in its entirety from the *Spirit-Filled
Life Bible* without revisions or deletions. Therefore, it may contain cross
references and study notes that point to other parts of the Bible. In addition, some notes may build from previous notes and/or point to other notes
outside of the Book of Acts. You may view a list of editors and contributors
and find a thorough description of the study tools found in this Bible at
www.ThomasNelsonBibles.com/spirit-filled-life-bible.

Again, this is simply a taste.

> *Oh, taste and see that the Lord is good;*
> *blessed is the man who trusts in Him!*
>
> —Psalm 34:8

INTRODUCTION

The waves of successive seasons of revival blessing throughout church history have left recurring high-water marks. These signs of the Holy Spirit's surgings across the earth and throughout time have, as a rule, been the result of God's signal use of anointed men, whose leadership not only was the spearhead making a holy penetration in their world, but whose name became the designation of that revival era. Accordingly, we note the strata of church history by the mention of names, such as Augustine, Aquinas, Luther, Calvin, Knox, Huss, Wesley, Finney, and Moody.

But with the opening of the twentieth century, from out of the wellsprings of the holiness tradition, a revival broke forth which is distinctive in two ways. First, the wave of renewal it gave rise to in the church internationally has not receded; rather, it has continued to roll forward and to engulf leaders and laity in every historic tradition and contemporary circle of Christianity. Second, this revival has not been characterized by the leadership of any primary personality to set its agenda or establish its style. One historian has referred to the Pentecostal-Charismatic revival as "a movement without a man," thereby noting the phenomenon that its broadening tide of influence is dynamically global and impacting in every sector of the church. No one can prescribe the movement's boundaries, none can inscribe his name upon it, and no one can describe it in any other way than by Peter's words at Pentecost: "This is what was spoken by the prophet Joel: '... and in the last days ... I will pour out of My Spirit on all flesh'" (Acts 2:16, 17).

As the waves of this renewal have spread, the common denominator of those it engulfs is not a doctrinal position as much as it is a mutual sharing in a new dynamic. This "new" is neither novel nor unprecedented, but simply a rekindling and release of the simplicity and power inherent in the New Testament church—the life and ministry of Jesus continuing in His body today after the manner of the Books of Acts. Because of this, it has characteristically been difficult to prepare a single study Bible to serve this broad community. Their convictions about the Person of Jesus Christ, His virgin birth, sinless life, atoning death, literal resurrection, and majestic ascension are essentially in agreement. Their view of the authority of the Word of God and its divine inspiration is absolute and uniformly the same. And their experience of the contemporary operations of the Holy Spirit—whose fullness, fruit, gifts, and works of power are welcomed and realized today as at the church's inception—is held in general accord. However, by reason of the breadth of their denominational backgrounds, a wide diversity characterizes this band. They will be found at all points of the spectrum on such issues as: (1) Calvinism contrasted with Arminianism; (2) Dispensationalism contrasted with Covenant theology; (3) Premillennial, Postmillennial, and Amillennial differences in prophetic interpretation; and (4) views and practices on the place and purpose of "speaking in tongues" with reference to the believer's initial infilling with the Holy Spirit.

The striking fact, given this widely diverse group, is that their movement together reflects not a lack of conviction about those points wherein they view Scripture and experience differently, but a response to the Holy Spirit's compulsion to give place to another overarching conviction. These leaders choose to let brotherly love prevail in the church, to seek peace and pursue it, and to acknowledge the prayer of our Lord Jesus "that they may be one." None of these lack biblical depth or theological conviction, but are people who realize that Ephesians 4:13's "unity of the faith" focuses our mutual "knowledge of the Son of God" and not our private textbooks. We meet at the table of communion—remembering Christ's cross through which we have all been redeemed; celebrating His body to which we have been called; and testifying to the power of His blood that has redeemed, washed, and justified us from our sins. It is there we have found oneness—under Jesus' lordship, and where we choose to stand together as more and more of His body grow toward *"a perfect man, to the measure of the stature of the fullness of Christ . . . speaking the truth in love"* (see Eph. 4:13–15).

From this broad context and at this point in God's dealings throughout Christ's church globally, we have come to study and to serve, hoping that this Bible may contribute to the ongoing stream of the Holy Spirit's workings today and tomorrow. The team of scholars, pastor-teachers, writers, and editors express gratitude to God and to the executive leadership of Thomas Nelson for the privilege of involvement in this historic project. The first edition of the *Spirit-Filled Life® Bible,* released in 1991, was the first of its kind, in which a broadly representative team from more than twenty denominations and independent fellowships were banded together to produce a study Bible integrating the Pentecostal-Charismatic viewpoint. In noting this, the Executive Editor and his associates wish to acknowledge the earlier efforts of several Pentecostal teachers and scholars who have provided study Bible resources prior to the landmark event the *Spirit-Filled Life® Bible* occasioned. While its uniqueness in scope and persons involved distinguishes this present work, it is with gratitude and humility that we salute that worthy group who preceded us in such efforts at leading the people of God into His Word at greater depth.

As Executive Editor, I offer my most respectful thanks to my Christian brothers and sisters who have accomplished the written and editorial work herein. Special personal acknowledgment is also appropriate to my son, Jack Hayford III, for his arduous labors in this project, as well as to Janet Kemp, Susanne Mahdi, Renee McCarter, and John Silver.

May God be pleased to multiply the fruit of the labor of all who have given themselves to present you, the reader-student, with this Bible. We commit this work to Him with the psalmist's prayer: "And let the beauty of the LORD our God be upon us, and establish the work of our hands for us; yes, establish the work of our hands" (Ps. 90:17).

Jack W. Hayford
Executive Editor

INTRODUCTORY ADDENDUM TO *THE SPIRIT-FILLED LIFE® BIBLE,* THIRD EDITION

With the release of the third edition of the *Spirit-Filled Life® Bible,* a distinct sense of humility is felt, for God has clearly chosen to bless our work as we prayed. Not only has this Bible study and ministry resource found acceptance among multitudes in all parts of the church today, but a constant stream of heartfelt remarks and correspondence has confirmed its personal usefulness and practical ministry value. The sum of the vast majority would distill to one testimony: *"This study Bible has deepened my life in Christ and my life in the Holy Spirit, helping me grow and increasing my effectiveness as a servant of Jesus."* For that, and for the fruit being multiplied in the church through the spiritual growth of its members and their ministry, we offer high praise to God.

This Bible's study resources rest on the foundations of the first *Spirit-Filled Life® Bible* and *The New Spirit-Filled Life® Bible,* and on the work of two exceptional men, Dr. Sam Middlebrook and Dr. Jerry Horner, who served diligently as Old and New Testament editors, respectively, of the first edition, and whose legacies are reflected in this new work. We also extend our special thanks to the new contributors to this edition—men and women whose collective contributions have added new layers of insight and broadened even further the scope of our pursuit. With these, we must acknowledge the superb editorial assistance and dedicated diligence of Caroline Erickson and Vicki Wilstermann in bringing the second edition to fruition, not to mention the splendid editorial group at Thomas Nelson. Blessings upon each of these!

In all, we are grateful to offer an enriching resource for any who love the Savior and His Word—a tool for any of the host of believers the Holy Spirit is increasingly blending from varied sectors of Christ's body. In deepened partnership and spiritual passion, may we pursue the final harvest together.

Jack W. Hayford
Executive Editor

PREFACE TO THE
NEW KING JAMES VERSION

To understand the heart behind the New King James Version, one need look no further than the stated intentions of the original King James scholars: "Not to make a new translation ... but to make a good one better." The New King James Version is a continuation of the labors of the King James translators, unlocking for today's readers the spiritual treasures found especially in the Authorized Version of the Holy Bible.

While seeking to maintain the excellent *form* of the traditional English Bible, special care has also been taken to preserve the work of *precision* which is the legacy of the King James translators.

Where new translation has been necessary, the most complete representation of the original has been rendered by considering the definition and usage of the Hebrew, Aramaic, and Greek words in their contexts. This translation principle, known as *complete equivalence*, seeks to preserve accurately all of the information in the text while presenting it in good literary form.

In addition to accuracy, the translators have also sought to maintain those lyrical and devotional qualities that are so highly regarded in the King James Version. The thought flow and selection of phrases from the King James Version have been preserved wherever possible without sacrificing clarity.

The format of the New King James Version is designed to enhance the vividness, devotional quality, and usefulness of the Bible. Words or phrases in italics indicate expressions in the original language that require clarification by additional English words, as was done in the King James Version. Poetry is structured as verse to reflect the form and beauty of the passage in the original language. The covenant name of God was usually translated from the Hebrew as LORD or GOD, using capital letters as shown, as in the King James Version. This convention is also maintained in the New King James Version when the Old Testament is quoted in the New.

The Hebrew text used for the Old Testament is the 1967/1977 Stuttgart edition of the *Biblia Hebraica*, with frequent comparisons to the Bomberg edition of 1524–25. Ancient versions and the Dead Sea Scrolls were consulted, but the Hebrew is followed wherever possible. Significant variations, explanations, and alternate renderings are mentioned in footnotes.

The Greek text used for the New Testament is the one that was followed by the King James translators: the traditional text of the Greek-speaking churches, called the Received Text or Textus Receptus, first published in 1516. Footnotes indicate significant variants from the Textus Receptus as found in two other editions of the Greek New Testament:

(1) NU-Text: These variations generally represent the Alexandrian or Egyptian text type as found in the critical text published in the twenty-seventh edition of the Nestle-Aland Greek New Testament (N) and in the United Bible Societies' third edition (U).

(2) M-Text: These variations represent readings found in the text of The Greek New Testament According to the Majority Text, which follows the consensus of the majority of surviving New Testament manuscripts.

The textual notes in the New King James Version make no evaluation, but objectively present the facts about variant readings.

ACTS

AUTHOR: Historically, Luke

DATE: About A.D. 62

THEMES: The Birth of the Early Church; The Power of the Holy Spirit Through the Church

KEY WORDS: Jesus, Holy Spirit, Believed, Baptized, Apostles, Church

AUTHOR

The Book of Acts does not specifically mention its author, but many indicators point to Luke, "the beloved physician" (Col. 4:14) who also wrote the Gospel of Luke. He was a close associate of Paul, as indicated in the "we" sections of the book. The writer was a man of culture, as indicated by his literary style; he had a universal outlook; and he revealed an interest in medical matters. In addition, church tradition uniformly declares that Luke authored Acts. Therefore, the bulk of the evidence, both external and internal, supports Luke as the author.

DATE

Luke tells the story of the early church within the framework of geographical, political, and historical details that could only fit in the first century. For example, Luke's use of regional Roman governmental titles, which only someone living at the time could know precisely, suggests that the book was probably written within its actual time frame. Furthermore, there is no mention of the fall of Jerusalem in A.D. 70 and Nero's persecution of the Christians, which began about A.D. 64. Therefore, because of these facts and because the book does not record Paul's death, it is logical to date the writing of Acts near the end of the apostle's imprisonment there in about A.D. 62.

CONTENT

Acts is a sequel to the life of Christ in the Gospels, and it records the spread of Christianity from Jerusalem to Rome. It tells how the apostles and early church leaders applied Jesus' Great Commission to make disciples of all nations (see Matt. 28:18–20; Luke 24:46–49).

Acts 1:8 is the key to the book. Not only does this verse prophesy the outpouring of the Spirit and its powerful witness, but its geographical references ("Jerusalem, and in all Judea and Samaria, and to the end of the earth") present a simple outline of the narrative. In general, Acts relates the step-by-step expansion of Christianity westward from Palestine to Italy. The book thus begins in Jerusalem (chs. 1–7), with Peter assuming the major role and Jews as the recipients of the gospel.

Following the death of Stephen (7:60—8:1), widespread persecution broke out against the church, and believers scattered, sowing the seed of the gospel in Samaria and among the Gentiles (chs. 8–12). During this period of history, Saul's conversion occurred (9:1–19), an event of such importance that Luke includes three descriptions of the incident (chs. 9; 22; 26).

The longest section of Acts focuses on the development and expansion of the Gentile ministry directed by Paul and his associates (chs. 13–28). It concludes with Paul's arrival in Rome, capital of the empire and representative of "the end of the earth" (1:8). The book ends rather abruptly because, in all likelihood, Luke had brought his narrative up-to-date and had nothing more to write.

PURPOSE

The key to the purpose of Acts is in the first verse, where Luke implies that the book is a continuation of his Gospel. The Gospel tells what "Jesus began both to do and teach," and Acts tells what the risen Lord continues to do and teach through the Holy Spirit.

PERSONAL APPLICATION

Acts shows us how to live under the power of the Holy Spirit, and it teaches us how to live together in meaningful Christian fellowship, sharing freely with one another (2:42; 4:32–35).

Conversely, Acts also shows that Christians inevitably will have disagreements (6:1; 11:1–3; 15:2, 7; 15:36–39), but that God gives us wisdom and grace to settle our differences (15:12–22). Even though the early church had its share of strong personalities, the people were willing to listen and to submit to one another (15:6–14), and we need to do the same in our time.

Probably the most prominent characteristic of the early Christians was their spiritual power. They fasted and prayed fervently (see 2:42; 6:4; 13:3), and their faith released the miracle-working power of God (see 3:16). Acts encourages us that ordinary people can do extraordinary things when empowered by the Holy Spirit. Many signs will follow those who believe (Mark 16:17, 18).

CHRIST REVEALED

The Book of Acts consistently records key apostolic proclamations of the gospel of Jesus Christ:

- Jesus is a historical figure, a Man empowered to perform signs and wonders (see 2:22; 10:38).
- Jesus' death can be attributed equally to human wickedness and to God's purpose. On the one hand, the Jews had "crucified" Him "by lawless hands" (2:23; see 3:13–15; 4:10; 5:30; 7:52; 10:39; 13:28). On the other hand, Jesus had been "delivered by the determined purpose and foreknowledge of God" (2:23; see 17:3).
- Jesus' resurrection fulfills Old Testament prophecy and demonstrates that God had reversed the death sentence proclaimed against Jesus by raising Him from the dead (1:3; 2:24–32; 4:10; 5:30; 10:40, 41; 13:30–37; 17:31).
- Jesus has been exalted to a position of unique and universal dominion (2:33–36; 3:21; 5:31). From that place of supreme honor and executive power, Jesus had poured out the promised Holy Spirit (2:33), who bears witness to Him (5:32) and empowers believers (1:8).
- Jesus has been "ordained by God to be Judge of the living and the dead" (10:42) and will return in triumph at the end of the age (1:11). Meanwhile, those who believe in Him will receive forgiveness of sins (2:21; 3:19; 4:12; 5:31; 10:43; 13:38, 39) and "the gift of the Holy Spirit" (2:38). Those who do not believe in Him are destined for terrible things (3:23).

THE HOLY SPIRIT AT WORK

The power of the Holy Spirit through the church is the most striking feature in Acts. The work of the Spirit in this book, however, cannot be understood without seeing the relationship between Acts and the Gospels, which demonstrates an essential continuity. Both the public ministry of Jesus in the Gospels and the public ministry of the church in Acts begin with a life-changing encounter with the Spirit; both are essential accounts of the results of that event.

The power of the Spirit in Jesus' life authorized Him to preach the kingdom of God and to demonstrate kingdom power by healing the sick, casting out demons, and setting the captives free (Luke 4:14–19; Matt. 4:23). The same Spirit power in Acts 2 gave the same authority to the disciples. *Jesus is the prototype of the Spirit-filled, Spirit-empowered life (10:38); the Book of Acts is the story of the disciples receiving what Jesus received in order to do what Jesus did.*

Luke's terminology in describing people's experience with the Holy Spirit in Acts is fluid. He is more interested in conveying a relational dynamic than in delineating a precisely worded theology. Note the different ways Luke describes people's encounter with the Spirit, which are all essential equivalents of Jesus' promise that the church would "be baptized with the Holy Spirit" (1:5; see its immediate fulfillment in 2:4):

- They were "filled with the Holy Spirit" (2:4; 9:17)
- "They received the Holy Spirit" (8:17)
- "The Holy Spirit fell upon [them]" (10:44)
- "The Holy Spirit had been poured out on [them]" (10:45)
- "The Holy Spirit came upon them" (19:6)

Three of these five instances record specific, special manifestations of the Spirit in which the people themselves participated. Those on the Day of Pentecost and the Gentiles of Cornelius' house spoke with other tongues (2:4; 10:46); the Ephesians "spoke with tongues and prophesied" (19:6). It is generally agreed that there was also some type of manifestation because Simon "saw" that the Holy Spirit had been given (8:18).

It can be rightly said that the Book of Acts is about the acts of the Holy Spirit who fills and empowers us.

OUTLINE OF ACTS

Prologue	**1:1–14**	C. Peter's explanatory sermon	2:14–39	
I. **Preface**	**1:1–3**	D. The new church after		
II. **Promise of the Holy Spirit**	**1:4–8**	Pentecost	2:40–47	
III. **Christ's Ascension**	**1:9–11**	III. **Healing of the Lame Man**	**3:1 – 4:31**	
IV. **Upper Room Prayer Meeting**	**1:12–14**	A. The healing miracle	3:1–10	
Part One: Peter and the Ministry of the		B. Peter's explanatory sermon	3:11–26	
Jewish Church in Jerusalem **1:15 – 12:24**		C. Arrest of Peter and John	4:1–4	
I. **Selection of Matthias as the**		D. Peter's defense before the		
Twelfth Apostle	**1:15–26**	Sanhedrin	4:5–12	
II. **Pentecostal Outpouring of the**		E. The Sanhedrin's response	4:13–22	
Holy Spirit	**2:1–47**	F. Thanksgiving for the apostles'		
A. Outpouring of the Spirit	2:1–4	release	4:23–31	
B. The crowd's confused response	2:5–13			

Prologue

1 The former account I made, O *a*Theophilus, of all that Jesus began both to do and teach, 2*a*until the day in which [1]He was taken up, after He through the Holy Spirit *b*had given commandments to the apostles whom He had chosen, 3*a*to whom He also presented Himself alive after His suffering by many [1]infallible proofs, being seen by them during forty days and speaking of the things pertaining to the kingdom of God.

The Holy Spirit Promised

4*a*And being assembled together with *them,* He commanded them not to depart from Jerusalem, but to wait for the *Promise of the Father, "which," *He said,* "you

KINGDOM DYNAMICS

1:5–8 The Baptism with the Holy Spirit, HOLY SPIRIT FULLNESS. This Ascension-day promise of Jesus to the assembled believers anticipates the Day of Pentecost and describes the coming of Pentecost as being "baptized with the Holy Spirit." This is not the same experience as described in John 20:22 ("Receive the Holy Spirit"). The experience in John 20:22 took place before the Ascension and was related to the work of the Holy Spirit in the New Birth as promised in John 3:3–5. Here in Acts 1:5 is the empowering for ministry that was promised in Luke 24:49. The focus here is on the mission of the believers—one that cannot be accomplished without the supernatural Holy Spirit baptism, which was to follow. Jesus' words about the spreading witness of the gospel through the Spirit-filled disciples in Acts 1:8 could only be fulfilled with supernatural power as a result of being baptized with the Holy Spirit. (John 20:22/Acts 2:4–13) S.G.B.

CHAPTER 1
1 *a*Luke 1:3
2 *a*Mark 16:19; Acts 1:9, 11, 22 *b*Matt. 28:19; Mark 16:15; John 20:21; Acts 10:42 [1]He ascended into heaven.
3 *a*Matt. 28:17; Mark 16:12, 14; Luke 24:34, 36; John 20:19, 26; 21:1, 14; 1 Cor. 15:5–7 [1]unmistakable
4 *a*Luke 24:49 *b*[John 14:16, 17, 26; 15:26]; Acts 2:33 *See WW at Acts 13:32.
5 *a*Matt. 3:11; Mark 1:8; Luke 3:16; John 1:33; Acts 11:16 *b*[Joel 2:28]
7 *a*1 Thess. 5:1 *b*Matt. 24:36; Mark 13:32 *See WW at Col. 4:5. • See WW at Mark 3:15.
8 *a*[Acts 2:1, 4] *b*Luke 24:49 *c*Luke 24:48; John 15:27 *d*Acts 8:1, 5, 14 *e*Matt. 28:19; Mark 16:15; Rom. 10:18; Col. 1:23; [Rev. 14:6] [1]NU *My witnesses*
9 *a*Luke 24:50, 51 *b*Ps. 68:18; 110:1; Mark 16:19; Luke 23:43; John 20:17; Acts 1:2; [Heb. 4:14; 9:24; 1 Pet. 3:22]
10 *a*Matt. 28:3; Mark 16:5; Luke 24:4; John 20:12; Acts 10:3, 30
11 *a*Dan. 7:13;

WORD WEALTH

1:7 times, *chronos;* Strong's #5550: Compare "chronology," "chronic," "chronicles." Duration of time, which may be a point, a lapse, a span, a period, a stretch, a quantity, a measure, a duration, or a length. *Kairos* ("seasons") suggests a kind of time. *Chronos* tells what day it is. *Kairos* tells of special happenings occurring during the time frame of *chronos.*

have *b*heard from Me; 5*a*for John truly baptized with water, *b*but you shall be baptized with the Holy Spirit not many days from now." 6Therefore, when they had come together, they asked Him, saying, "Lord, will You at this time restore the kingdom to Israel?" 7And He said to them, *a*"It is not for you to *b*know **times** or *seasons which the Father has put in His own *authority. 8*a*But you shall receive power *b*when the Holy Spirit has come upon you; and *c*you shall be [1]witnesses to Me in Jerusalem, and in all Judea and *d*Samaria, and to the *e*end of the earth." ②

Jesus Ascends to Heaven

9*a*Now when He had spoken these things, while they watched, *b*He was taken up, and a cloud received Him out of their sight. 10And while they looked steadfastly toward heaven as He went up, behold, two men stood by them *a*in white apparel, 11who also said, "Men of Galilee, why do you stand gazing up into *heaven? This *same* Jesus, who was taken up from you into heaven, *a*will so come in like manner as you saw Him go into heaven."

Mark 13:26; Luke 21:27; [John 14:3]; 2 Thess. 1:10; Rev. 1:7 *See WW at Rev. 21:1.

1:1 The former account refers to the Gospel of Luke. **Theophilus** is the unknown recipient. His name means "Loved by God," and in Luke 1:3 he is called "most excellent," a formal title of respect. Physicians like Luke (Col. 4:14) were often slaves. Theophilus may have been Luke's former master. Luke's **began** intimates that Acts records the dynamic kingdom teaching and ministry of Jesus that the church continues to do. See note on 1:3; Kingdom Dynamics at Luke 9:1, 2.

1:2 Acts reveals the transfer of Christ's authority and mission to His disciples. **Apostles** here refers to the founding apostles (see note on Eph. 2:20). See note on Acts 1:22.

1:3 Alive . . . by many infallible proofs: The Resurrection of Christ is the bedrock of Christianity and the initiating event of Acts (2:32, 33). **The kingdom of God,** the divine rule in human hearts, lives, and situations, was a prominent theme in Jesus' teaching. Jesus began to do and teach the kingdom through the Spirit's power (Luke 4:18, 19), and He is about to transfer that power and responsibility to His disciples by baptizing them in the same Spirit that had authorized His ministry. See Kingdom Dynamics at Mark 1:14, 15.

1:5 You shall be baptized with the Holy Spirit is the source of the phrase "the baptism 'in' or 'with' the Holy Spirit." Acts has many synonyms for this dynamic. See Introduction to Acts: The Holy Spirit at Work. Many understand this as a work distinct

from conversion, which is seen as being referred to in 1 Cor. 12:3, where the Holy Spirit is the Agent performing the baptizing work. See notes on Acts 2:4; 1 Cor. 12:13, and Holy Spirit Gifts and Power: How Can Spiritual Integrity Be Maintained in the Midst of It?

1:6 The disciples are still thinking of the messianic kingdom in terms of political power.

1:7, 8 In His reply Jesus corrects their misconception and adjusts their perspective concerning the kingdom of God. He declares that the kingdom is currently spiritual in its character, international in its membership, and gradual in its expansion. **The Holy Spirit . . . upon** one is an important concept in Luke and Acts, and Jesus is a primary example of the work of the Holy Spirit *within* and *upon* us. Jesus' life was conceived by the Spirit, and the Spirit working *within* Him brought forth the fruit of good character (Luke 2:52). Later the Spirit came *upon* Jesus to bring forth a ministry of power (Luke 3:22; 4:18). The distinctive purpose of the outpouring of the Spirit in Acts is to empower the church for ministry. See Introduction to Acts: The Holy Spirit at Work.

1:8 See section 2 of Truth in Action at the end of Acts.

1:9 The **cloud** is likely a reference to the radiant cloud of God's special glory, the Shekinah (see Matt. 17:5).

1:11 Will so come in like manner: Jesus will return bodily, literally.

The Upper Room Prayer Meeting

12 [a]Then they returned to Jerusalem from the mount called Olivet, which is near Jerusalem, a Sabbath day's journey. 13 And when they had entered, they went up [a]into the upper room where they were staying: [b]Peter, James, John, and Andrew; Philip and Thomas; Bartholomew and Matthew; James *the son* of Alphaeus and [c]Simon the Zealot; and [d]Judas *the son* of James. 14 [a]These all continued *with one [l]accord in prayer [2]and supplication, with [b]the women and Mary the mother of Jesus, and with [c]His brothers.

Matthias Chosen

15 And in those days Peter stood up in the midst of the [l]disciples (altogether the number [a]of names was about a hundred and twenty), and said, 16 "Men *and* brethren, this *Scripture had to be fulfilled, [a]which the Holy Spirit spoke before by the mouth of David concerning Judas, [b]who became a guide to those who arrested Jesus; 17 for [a]he was numbered with us and obtained a part in [b]this ministry."

18 [a](Now this man purchased a field with [b]the [l]wages* of iniquity; and falling headlong, he burst open in the middle and all his [2]entrails gushed out. 19 And it became known to all those dwelling in Jerusalem; so that field is called in their own language, Akel Dama, that is, Field of Blood.)

20 "For it is written in the Book of Psalms:

[a]'Let his dwelling place be [l]desolate,
And let no one live in it';

and,

[b]'Let another take his [2]office.'

21 "Therefore, of these men who have accompanied us all the time that the Lord Jesus went in and out among us, 22 beginning from the *baptism of John to that

day when [a]He was taken up from us, one of these must [b]become a *witness with us of His *resurrection."

23 And they proposed two: Joseph called [a]Barsabas, who was surnamed Justus, and Matthias. 24 And they prayed and said, "You, O Lord, [a]who know the hearts of all, show which of these two You have chosen 25 [a]to take part in this ministry and apostleship from which Judas by **transgression** fell, that he might go to his own place." 26 And they cast their lots, and the lot fell on Matthias. And he was numbered with the eleven *apostles.

Coming of the Holy Spirit

2 When [a]the Day of Pentecost had fully come, [b]they were all [l]with one accord in one place. 2 And suddenly there came a sound from *heaven, as of a rushing mighty wind, and [a]it filled the whole house where they were sitting. 3 Then there appeared to

Cross references (center column)

12 [a]Luke 24:52
13 [a]Mark 14:15;
Luke 22:12;
Acts 9:37, 39;
20:8 [b]Matt.
10:2–4 [c]Luke
6:15 [d]Jude 1
14 [a]Acts 2:1, 46
[b]Luke 23:49,
55 [c]Matt.
13:55 [l]purpose
or mind [2]NU
omits and
supplication
*See WW at
Acts 2:1.
15 [a]Luke 22:32;
Rev. 3:4 [l]NU
brethren
16 [a]Ps. 41:9
[b]Matt. 26:47;
Mark 14:43;
Luke 22:47;
John 18:3
*See WW at
John 5:39.
17 [a]Matt. 10:4
[b]Acts 1:25
18 [a]Matt.
27:3–10 [b]Matt.
18:7; 26:14,
15, 24; Mark
14:21; Luke
22:22; John
17:12 [l]reward
of unrigh-
teousness
[2]intestines
*See WW at Rev.
22:12.
20 [a]Ps. 69:25
[b]Ps. 109:8
[l]deserted [2]Gr.
episkopen,
position of
overseer
22 [a]Acts 1:9
[b]Acts 1:8;
2:32
*See WW at Matt.
21:25. • See
WW at Acts
1:5. • See WW
at Acts 23:6.
23 [a]Acts 15:22
24 [a]1 Sam. 16:7;
Jer. 17:10;
Acts 1:2
25 [a]Acts 1:17
26 *See WW at
1 Cor. 12:28.

CHAPTER 2
1 [a]Lev. 23:15;
Deut. 16:9;
Acts 20:16;
1 Cor. 16:8
[b]Acts 1:14 [l]NU
together
2 [a]Acts 4:31
*See WW at Rev.
21:1.

1:12 The mount called Olivet was just outside Jerusalem, overlooking the city from the east. **A Sabbath day's journey** was about ¾ mile.

1:14 Fervent and persistent prayer is prominent in Acts. Here the prayer is an obedient response to Jesus' command to wait in Jerusalem (v. 4).

1:15 The phrase Peter stood up points to the beginning of Peter's formal leadership and the first major section of the book.

1:18 There is no discrepancy with Matt. 27:5–10. The priests, considering the bribe money paid to Judas to be his legal property, **purchased the field** in his name. After Judas hanged himself, his body fell when the rope broke or was cut by someone. Luke describes the gruesome results of the suicide.

1:22 A witness . . . of His resurrection was the essential requirement for serving as one of the original 12 apostles. These, of course, have died, but the general ministry of apostleship remains (Eph. 4:11).

1:26 Casting lots was a provision of the Law (Lev. 16:8). It may

be significant that following the outpouring of the Holy Spirit at Pentecost there is no more mention of the practice. Notice also that on this occasion the disciples first selected the two men they judged most worthy to fill the vacancy. The final decision was left to the Lord as they prayed (Acts 1:24). To be certain of His will they cast lots. Afterward the Holy Spirit provided the needed guidance.

2:1 Pentecost was an annual Jewish festival, also known as the "Feast of Weeks," or the "Day of Firstfruits," a celebration of the first buds of the harvest. Jewish men were required by law to go to Jerusalem three times each year to celebrate the major feasts (Deut. 16:16): Passover in the spring; Pentecost (Gr. *pentēkostē*, "fiftieth") seven weeks and a day later (Lev. 23:15, 16); and Tabernacles at the end of the harvest in the fall. Lev. 23 details the dates and rituals of the Jewish festival calendar. Those who became Christians on Pentecost were the firstfruits of a vast harvest of millions of souls.

2:2 As of a rushing mighty wind: Not a wind, but like the sound of a wind (see John 3:8), suggesting the mighty but unseen power of the Spirit.

them ¹divided tongues, as of fire, and *one*
② sat upon each of them. ⁴And ªthey were all
filled with the Holy Spirit and began ᵇto
speak with other tongues, as the Spirit gave
them utterance.

3 ¹Or *tongues as of fire, distributed and resting on each*
4 ªMatt. 3:11; 5:6; 10:20; Luke 3:16; John 14:16;

The Crowd's Response

⁵And there were dwelling in Jerusalem
Jews, ªdevout men, from every nation under

16:7–15; Acts 1:5 ᵇMark 16:17; Acts 10:46; 19:6; [1 Cor. 12:10, 28, 30; 13:1] **5** ªLuke 2:25; Acts 8:2

2:3 Tongues, as of fire: Not fire, but like fire. John the Baptist foretold how Spirit baptism would be accompanied by wind and fire (Matt. 3:11, 12). This may also be an allusion to the burning bush (Ex. 3:2–5), which was a symbol of the divine presence. This outward manifestation of the Spirit's coming was another sign of His power.

2:4 See section 2 of Truth in Action at the end of Acts.

2:4 This is the initial fulfillment of Jesus' promise in 1:5, 8. The interchangeable terms in each of the three references is common to Acts. See Introduction to Acts: The Holy Spirit at Work. The OT expectation about the coming of the Spirit and the beginning of a new era is at last fulfilled. **Other tongues** here refers to spoken human languages, unknown to the speakers but known by others (v. 6); a distinct practice of the Spirit's fullness that evolved at some later point in the development of the church, is that of speaking "with the [unknown] tongues . . . of angels" (1 Cor. 13:1). **Began to speak** indicates that they continued in the process (see Acts 11:15). Luke could be indicating that they continued speaking for an extended time; more likely, however, he is indicating that this practice continued in their lives, just as he records the church's continuation of what Jesus "began both to do and to teach" (1:1).

Many contemporary Christians from all denominational backgrounds believe that the phenomenon of "speaking with tongues" or speaking in a spiritual language (language the speaker has not formerly learned or known by) may accompany a person's initial surrender to the fullness of the Holy Spirit. In classical Pentecostal tradition, this experience is expected and is doctrinally expressed in the words, "The initial physical evidence of the baptism with the Holy Spirit is speaking with other tongues."

Other Christians and many Charismatics who do not accept this doctrinal terminology still apply its fundamental implications in their practice. This modified view, which some Pentecostals also accept, places less emphasis on the importance of tongues or spiritual language as the evidence of the baptism with the Holy Spirit, either in terms of one's initial experience or one's ongoing life of Spirit fullness. These focus more on all the gifts, with speaking in tongues seen as but one of them, since all the gifts are deemed contemporarily operational and any one of them may serve as a sign of one's baptism in the Spirit. Further, one's deepened participation in worship is also seen as a fundamental indication of being baptized in the Spirit, with the continual exercise of spiritual language as a part of the believer's private devotional expression (see 1 Cor. 14:1, 2, 4, 15, 39, 40).

Some other Christians who disagree with the above views usually explain the baptism with the Holy Spirit in one of the following ways: (a) as an experience subsequent to salvation, bringing needed divine power for Christian witness and service, but without any expectation of the Holy Spirit's gifts attending this experience; (b) as exclusively synonymous with one's conversion experience, when the Holy Spirit merges the individual into the body of Christ at the time the believer places personal faith in Jesus as Lord (see note on 1 Cor. 12:3); and (c) as unique to the Book of Acts, claiming the baptism with the Holy Spirit, including its miraculous manifestations, was solely a singular event of a single divine outpouring, first at Pentecost, though repeated at later junctures, when the ethnic barriers of the Samaritans (ch. 8) and Gentiles (ch. 10) were breached.

2:5 These international Jews had made the pilgrimage to Jerusalem to celebrate the festival of Pentecost (see note on v. 1).

THE NATIONS OF PENTECOST

ASIA – Provinces of the Roman Empire
Media – Provinces of the Parthian Empire
Rome – Cities
CRETE – Island
(1) (2) (3) etc. – Numbers indicate sequence listed in Acts 2:9–11

0   300 km.
0   300 miles

In the first century, Jewish communities were located primarily in the eastern part of the Roman Empire, where Greek was the common language, but also existed as far west as Italy and as far east as Babylonia.

KINGDOM DYNAMICS

2:4–13 The Miracle of Pentecost, HOLY SPIRIT FULLNESS. The miracle of Pentecost happened to everyone in the Upper Room: "They were all filled with the Holy Spirit and began to speak with other tongues" (v. 4). The 120 gathered in the Upper Room without an expectation of what would happen—only that they should stay there until it did. Some propose that the languages spoken on the Day of Pentecost were _all_ known languages; however, there is no support for this in the text. First, those filled with the Spirit that day did not know the languages that they began speaking, though about a dozen of

those languages understood were identified by visitors attending the feast in Jerusalem. Second, since all 120 spoke with tongues, it is logical and likely that many other unidentified languages were spoken—all, doubtless, in the same spirit of worshiping God's "wonderful works" (v. 11). The result: The church was birthed in the worshiping, ministering power of the Holy Spirit; and shortly, three thousand people received Christ. This enablement by the Spirit initiated the spread of the gospel in the hostile environment of persecution, idolatry, and political oppression, and it is still the answer for the spread of the gospel today. (Acts 1:5–8/Acts 8:14) S.G.B.

6 ªActs 4:32
7 ªMatt. 26:73; Acts 1:11
8 ¹dialect
9 ª1 Pet. 1:1
11 ¹Arabians

heaven. 6And when this sound occurred, the ªmultitude came together, and were confused, because everyone heard them speak in his own language. 7Then they were all amazed and marveled, saying to one another, "Look, are not all these who speak ªGalileans? 8And how _is it that_ we hear, each in our own ¹language in which we were born? 9Parthians and Medes and Elamites, those dwelling in Mesopotamia, Judea and ªCappadocia, Pontus and Asia, 10Phrygia and Pamphylia, Egypt and the parts of Libya adjoining Cyrene, visitors from Rome, both Jews and proselytes, 11Cretans and ¹Arabs—we hear them speaking in our own tongues the **wonderful works** of God." 12So they were all amazed and perplexed, saying to one another, "Whatever could this mean?"

THE WORK OF THE HOLY SPIRIT (2:4)

In the beginning
- Active and present at creation, hovering over the unordered conditions (Gen. 1:2)

In the Old Testament
- The origin of supernatural abilities (Gen. 41:38)
- The giver of artistic skill (Ex. 31:2–5)
- The source of power and strength (Judg. 3:9, 10)
- The inspiration of prophecy (1 Sam. 19:20, 23)
- The equipper of God's messenger (Mic. 3:8)

In Old Testament prophecy
- The cleansing of the heart for holy living (Ezek. 36:25–29)

In salvation
- Brings conviction (John 16:8–11)
- Regenerates the believer (Titus 3:5)
- Sanctifies the believer (2 Thess. 2:13)
- Completely indwells the believer (John 14:17; Rom. 8:9–11)

In the New Testament
- Imparts spiritual truth (John 14:26; 16:13; 1 Cor. 2:13–15)
- Glorifies Christ (John 16:14)
- Endows with power for Good News proclamation (Acts 1:8)
- Fills believers (Acts 2:4)
- Pours out God's love in the heart (Rom. 5:5)
- Enables believers to walk in holiness (Rom. 8:1–8; Gal. 5:16–25)
- Makes intercession (Rom. 8:26)
- Imparts gifts for ministry (1 Cor. 12:4–11)
- Strengthens the inner being (Eph. 3:16)

In the written Word
- Inspired the writing of Scripture (2 Tim. 3:16; 2 Pet. 1:21)

WORD WEALTH

2:11 wonderful works, *megaleios;* (Strong's #3167: Conspicuous, magnificent, splendid, majestic, sublime, grand, beautiful, excellent, favorable. Used here and in Luke 1:49. The amazed visitors at Pentecost heard the disciples in their own languages reciting the sublime greatness of God and His mighty deeds.

13Others mocking said, "They are full of new wine."

Peter's Sermon

14But Peter, standing up with the eleven, raised his voice and said to them, "Men of Judea and all who dwell in Jerusalem, let this be known to you, and heed my words. 15For these are not drunk, as you suppose, ªsince it is *only* ¹the third hour of the day. 16But this is what was spoken by the prophet Joel:

17 'Andª it shall come to pass in the last days, says God,
ᵇThat I will pour out of My Spirit on all *flesh;
Your sons and ᶜyour daughters shall prophesy,
Your young men shall see visions,
Your old men shall dream dreams.
18 And on My menservants and on My maidservants
I will pour out My Spirit in those days;
ªAnd they shall prophesy.
19 ªI will show *wonders in heaven above
And signs in the earth beneath:
Blood and fire and vapor of smoke.
20 ªThe sun shall be turned into darkness,
And the moon into blood,
Before the coming of the great and awesome day of the LORD.
21 And it shall come to pass
That ªwhoever calls on the name of the LORD
Shall be saved.'

22"Men of Israel, hear these words: *Jesus of Nazareth, a Man attested by God to you

---

Cross references (center column):

15 ª1 Thess. 5:7
¹9 A.M.
17 ªIs. 44:3; Ezek. 11:19; Joel 2:28–32; [Zech. 12:10; John 7:38]
ᵇActs 10:45
ᶜActs 21:9
*See WW at Matt. 26:41.
18 ªActs 21:4, 9; 1 Cor. 12:10
19 ªJoel 2:30
*See WW at Acts 15:12.
20 ªIs. 13:10; Ezek. 32:7; Matt. 24:29; Mark 13:24, 25; Luke 21:25; Rev. 6:12
21 ªRom. 10:13
22 *See WW at Phil. 4:23.

ªIs. 50:5; John 3:2; 5:6; Acts 10:38
*See WW at Rev. 16:14.
23 ªMatt. 26:4; Luke 22:22; Acts 3:18; 4:28; [1 Pet. 1:20] ᵇActs 5:30 ¹NU omits have taken
24 ª[Rom. 8:11; 1 Cor. 6:14; 2 Cor. 4:14; Eph. 1:20; Col. 2:12]; 1 Thess. 1:10; Heb. 13:20 ¹destroyed or abolished ²Lit. birth pangs
25 ªPs. 16:8–11
27 ªActs 13:30–37
29 ªActs 13:36
30 ª2 Sam. 7:12; Ps. 132:11; Luke 1:32; Rom. 1:3; 2 Tim. 2:8 ¹NU He would seat one on his throne,
31 ªPs. 16:10; Is. 50:8; 53:10
*See WW at 2 Tim. 4:22.
32 ªActs 2:24 ᵇActs 1:8; 3:15
33 ªPs. 68:18; [Acts 5:31]; Phil. 2:9 ᵇPs. 110:1; Mark 16:19; [Heb. 10:12] ᶜLuke 24:49; [John 14:26] ᵈMatt. 3:11; 5:6;

ªby miracles, wonders, and *signs which God did through Him in your midst, as you yourselves also know— 23Him, ªbeing delivered by the determined purpose and foreknowledge of God, ᵇyou ¹have taken by lawless hands, have crucified, and put to death; 24ªwhom God raised up, having ¹loosed the ²pains of death, because it was not possible that He should be held by it. 25For David says concerning Him:

ª'I foresaw the LORD always before my face,
For He is at my right hand, that I may not be shaken.
26 Therefore my heart rejoiced, and my tongue was glad;
Moreover my flesh also will rest in hope.
27 For You will not leave my soul in Hades,
Nor will You allow Your Holy One to see ªcorruption.
28 You have made known to me the ways of life;
You will make me full of joy in Your presence.'

29"Men *and* brethren, let *me* speak freely to you ªof the patriarch David, that he is both dead and buried, and his tomb is with us to this day. 30Therefore, being a prophet, ªand knowing that God had sworn with an oath to him that of the fruit of his body, ¹according to the flesh, He would raise up the Christ to sit on his throne, 31he, foreseeing this, spoke concerning the resurrection of the *Christ, ªthat His soul was not left in Hades, nor did His flesh see corruption. 32ªThis Jesus God has raised up, ᵇof which we are all witnesses. 33Therefore ªbeing exalted ¹to ᵇthe right hand of God, and ᶜhaving received from the Father the *promise of the Holy Spirit, He ᵈpoured out this which you now see and hear.

34"For David did not ascend into the heavens, but he says himself:

Luke 3:16; 22:69; John 14:16; 16:7–15; Acts 2:1–11, 17; 10:45; Eph. 4:8 ¹Possibly *by* *See WW at Acts 13:32.

2:13 The mockers apparently formed this conclusion from the fact that they did not recognize some of the sounds or from the fact that there was possible misunderstood ecstatic behavior.

2:14 Peter is the spokesman for the disciples and takes the lead role in Acts at this point.

2:15 The third hour of the day was about 9:00 A.M.

2:17, 18 The last days refer to the era of the church from Pentecost to the return of Christ (see Heb. 1:1, 2). They are an overlap of this age and the age to come. **I will pour out of My Spirit on all flesh:** Peter explains the unusual events of Pentecost in terms of the outpouring of the Spirit predicted in Joel's messianic word. The outpouring of the Spirit in the OT had been largely reserved for the spiritual and national leaders of Israel. Under the New Covenant, however, the authority of the Spirit is for "all flesh," all who come under the New Covenant. Every

believer is anointed to be a priest and king to God. Important evidences of participation in the Spirit's outpouring are **dreams** and prophecies.

2:19–21 Joel prophesied that this present age would end amidst mighty portents and in divine judgment, but that **whoever calls on the name of the LORD shall be saved.** Peter will proceed to establish that Jesus is the Lord who will return in judgment and upon whom people must now call in repentance and faith.

2:29–32 Peter proves that the Resurrection of Christ is foretold in the OT. Thus, his Jewish audience should readily accept Jesus as their Messiah.

2:33 See note on John 7:39.

2:34–36 The outpouring of the Spirit is a sign that Jesus has been exalted to the right hand of the Father. Pentecost is a sign that Jesus is Lord.

PRAYING THE WORD

Thank You, Lord, for the gift of repentance and the sacrament of baptism in the name of Your Son, Jesus Christ. Thank You for the gift of the Holy Spirit—the promise given to me, to my children, and to all who are afar off, as many as You will call.

Adapted from Acts 2:38, 39

a"The LORD said to my Lord,
"Sit at My right hand,
35 Till I make Your enemies Your
footstool." '

36"Therefore let all the house of Israel know assuredly that God has made this Jesus, whom you crucified, both Lord and Christ."

37Now when they heard *this,* *a*they were cut to the heart, and said to Peter and the rest of the apostles, "Men *and* brethren, what shall we do?"

① 38Then Peter said to them, *a*"Repent,* and let every one of you be baptized in the name of Jesus Christ for the *l*remission of sins; and you shall receive the gift of the Holy Spirit. 39For the promise is to you and *a*to your children, and *b*to all who are afar off, as many as the Lord our God will call."

A Vital Church Grows

40And with many *other words he testified and exhorted them, saying, "Be saved from this *l*perverse generation." 41Then those who *l*gladly received his word were baptized; and that day about three thou-
③ sand *souls were added *to them. 42*a*And they continued steadfastly in the apostles'

Cross references (center column):
34 *a*Ps. 68:18; 110:1; Matt. 22:44; Luke 23:43; John 20:17; 1 Cor. 15:25; Eph. 1:20; Heb. 1:13
37 *a*[Zech. 12:10]; Luke 3:10, 12, 14; John 16:8
38 *a*Luke 24:47 *l*forgiveness *See WW at Matt. 3:2.
39 *a*Joel 2:28, 32 *b*Acts 11:15, 18; Eph. 2:13
40 *l*crooked *See WW at Acts 4:12.
41 *l*NU omits gladly *See WW at Luke 21:19.
42 *a*Acts 1:14; Rom. 12:12; Eph. 6:18; Col. 4:2; Heb. 10:25

*l*teaching
43 *a*Mark 16:17; Acts 2:22 *See WW at 1 John 4:18.
44 *a*Acts 4:32, 34, 37; 5:2
45 *l*would sell

WORD WEALTH

2:42 fellowship, *koinōnia;* Strong's #2842: Sharing, unity, close association, partnership, participation, a society, a communion, a fellowship, contributory help, the brotherhood. (Compare "coin," "cenobite," "epicene.") *Koinōnia* is a unity brought about by the Holy Spirit. In *koinonia* the individual shares in common an intimate bond of fellowship with the rest of the Christian society. *Koinōnia* cements the believers to the Lord Jesus and to each other.

KINGDOM DYNAMICS

2:42 Fellowship (*koinōnia*), POWER OF UNITY. This first detailed description of the early Christians is wonderfully revealing. The followers of Jesus, who had been baptized by the Holy Spirit, literally devoted themselves to communication and unity with God and with each other. In relationship to God, they "continued steadfastly" in the apostles' doctrine (the Word of God) and in prayer. In relationship to one another, they devoted themselves to fellowship and to breaking bread with one another. As the Word Wealth article on this passage states, the word *koinōnia* literally denotes a deep sense of spiritual unity—of spiritual communion with the Lord and with each other. With the coming of the baptism of the Holy Spirit, the priorities of the followers of Christ focused upon spiritual unity with their Lord and with their brothers and sisters in Christ—within the church—the spiritual body of Christ. Every true Christian is a member of the body of Christ and is related to Christ and to other believers as a member of that body. This is the essence of true spiritual unity—the unity of the Spirit. (Ps. 133:1/ Acts 4:24) P.A.C.

*l*doctrine and **fellowship,** in the breaking of bread, and in prayers. 43Then *fear came upon every soul, and *a*many wonders and signs were done through the apostles. 44Now all who believed were together, and *a*had all things in common, 45and *l*sold their

---

2:38–41 See section 1 of Truth in Action at the end of Acts.

2:38 Peter calls upon his audience to change their opinion of and attitude toward Christ and to **be baptized in the name of Jesus Christ** as a public acknowledgment that they had accepted Jesus as Messiah and Lord. "Name" suggested nature or character; therefore, to be baptized "in the name of Jesus" is to confess Him to be all that His name denotes. Baptism in and of itself is not a means of forgiveness and salvation (see 3:19). For the early church, however, there was no separation between ritual and reality. Coming to Christ and being baptized were mutually inclusive. See 22:16; Mark 16:16; 1 Pet. 3:21. **The gift of the Holy Spirit** must be distinguished from the gifts of the Spirit (see text and notes on Rom. 12:6–8; 1 Cor. 12:1–31; Eph. 4:11). The former is the Holy Spirit Himself, while the latter are special abilities granted by the Spirit to equip believers for service (see 1 Cor. 12:1–31).

2:39 The promise of the Holy Spirit (see v. 33; 1:4, 5; Luke 24:49) is a gift for every believer in every generation. **All who are afar off** includes Gentiles (see Is. 57:19; Eph. 2:13, 17). Peter's words clearly extend to every believer in every era and everywhere, full reason to expect the same resource and experience that was afforded the first believers who received the Holy Spirit at the birth of the church.

2:42–47 See section 3 of Truth in Action at the end of Acts.

2:42 These are four fundamental devotions of the church throughout this age. **The breaking of bread** is probably a reference to the Lord's Supper in conjunction with a full meal.

2:43 Fear is not terror, but awe.

2:44, 45 This was spontaneous and voluntary benevolence as a result of truly understanding God's love. Forced community is communism.

possessions and goods, and [a]divided[2] them among all, as anyone had need.

46[a]So continuing daily *with one accord [b]in the temple, and [c]breaking bread from house to house, they ate their food with gladness and simplicity of heart, 47praising God and having favor with all the people. And [a]the Lord added [l]to the *church daily those who were being saved.

A Lame Man Healed

3 Now Peter and John went up together [a]to the temple at the hour of prayer, [b]the ninth *hour*. 2And [a]a certain man lame from his mother's womb was carried, whom they laid daily at the gate of the temple which is called Beautiful, [b]to [l]ask* alms from those who entered the temple; 3who, seeing Peter and John about to go into the temple, asked for alms. 4And fixing his eyes on him, with John, Peter said, "Look at us." 5So he gave them his attention, expecting to receive something from them. 6Then Peter said, "Silver and gold I do not have, but what I do have I give you: [a]In the *name of Jesus Christ of Nazareth, rise up and walk." 7And he took him by the right hand and lifted *him* up, and immediately his feet and ankle bones received *strength. 8So he, [a]leaping up, stood and walked and entered the temple with them—walking, leaping, and praising God. 9 [a]And all the people saw him walking and praising God. 10Then they knew that it was he who [a]sat begging alms at the Beautiful Gate of the temple; and they were filled with wonder and amazement at what had happened to him.

Preaching in Solomon's Portico

11Now as the lame man who was healed held on to Peter and John, all the people ran together to them in the porch [a]which is called Solomon's, greatly amazed. 12So when Peter saw *it*, he responded to the people: "Men of Israel, why do you marvel at this? Or why look so intently at us, as though by our own power or godliness we had made this man walk? 13[a]The God of Abraham, Isaac, and Jacob, the God of our fathers, [b]glorified His Servant Jesus,

whom you [c]delivered* up and [d]denied in the presence of Pilate, when he was determined to let *Him* go. 14But you denied [a]the Holy One [b]and the *Just, and [c]asked for a murderer to be granted to you, 15and killed the [l]Prince of life, [a]whom God raised from the dead, [b]of which we are witnesses. 16[a]And His name, through faith in His name, has made this man strong, whom you see and know. Yes, the faith which *comes* through Him has given him this perfect soundness in the presence of you all.

17"Yet now, brethren, I know that [a]you did *it* in ignorance, as *did* also your rulers. 18But [a]those things which God foretold [b]by the mouth of all His prophets, that the Christ would suffer, He has thus fulfilled. 19[a]Repent therefore and be converted, ① that your sins may be *blotted out, so that times of refreshing may come from the presence of the Lord, 20and that He may send [l]Jesus Christ, who was [2]preached to you before, 21[a]whom heaven must receive ④

45 [a]Is. 58:7
[2]distributed
46 [a]Acts 1:14
[b]Luke 24:53
[c]Luke 24:30;
Acts 2:42;
20:7; [1 Cor.
10:16]
*See WW at
Acts 2:1.
47 [a]Acts 5:14
[l]NU omits to
the church
*See WW at
Acts 8:1.

CHAPTER 3
1 [a]Acts 2:46 [b]Ps.
55:17; Matt.
27:45; Acts
10:30
2 [a]Acts 14:8
[b]John 9:8;
Acts 3:10
[l]Beg
*See WW at
Matt. 7:7.
6 [a]Acts 4:10
*See WW at
John 12:13.
7 *See WW at
Col. 2:5.
8 [a]Is. 35:6
9 [a]Acts 4:16, 21
10 [a]John 9:8;
Acts 3:2
11 [a]John 10:23;
Acts 5:12
13 [a]John 5:30
[b]Is. 49:3; John
7:39; 12:23;
13:31 [c]Matt.
27:2 [d]Matt.
27:20; Mark
15:11; Luke
23:18; John
18:40; Acts
13:28
*See WW at
Luke 23:25.
14 [a]Ps. 16:10;
Mark 1:24;
Luke 1:35
[b]Acts 7:52;
2 Cor. 5:21
[c]John 18:40
*See WW at
Matt. 1:19.
15 [a]Acts 2:24
[b]Acts 2:32 [l]Or
Originator
16 [a]Matt. 9:22;
Acts 4:10;
14:9
17 [a]Luke 23:34;
John 16:3;
[Acts 13:27;
17:30]; 1 Cor.
2:8; 1 Tim.
1:13
18 [a]Luke 24:44;
Acts 26:22 [b]Ps.
22; Is. 50:6;
53:5; Dan.
9:26; Hos. 6:1;
Zech. 13:6;
1 Pet. 1:10
19 [a][Acts 2:38;
26:20]
*See WW at Col.
2:14.
20 [l]NU, M Christ Jesus [2]NU, M ordained for you before
21 [a]Acts 1:11

3:1 At this early point in the history of the church, the Jewish Christians were still praying in **the temple. The ninth hour** was about 3:00 P.M.

3:6 This healing is a demonstration of either the manifestation of the gifts of healings or of the working of miracles (1 Cor. 12:9, 10). It is an example of the church continuing the kind of healing Jesus did (see Mark 2:1–12). See Kingdom Dynamics on Acts 28:8, 9.

3:12–26 Most of the sermons in Acts contain four elements: (1) a proclamation that the age of the Messiah has finally come; (2) quotations from the OT to prove that Jesus is the Messiah; (3) a review of the life and ministry of Jesus, especially His resurrection; and (4) a call to repentance.

3:16 Healing is by **faith in** the **name** of Jesus. In the cultural setting of the Bible, a name could not be separated from the person bearing that name, and the very name "Jesus Christ" means "Anointed Savior." Therefore, Peter is saying that it was the Messiah in all His fullness who healed the man. Furthermore, the miracle power was not in Peter's faith, but by **the faith which comes through Him** (see Heb. 12:2).

3:19, 20 See section 1 of Truth in Action at the end of Acts.

3:21 See section 4 of Truth in Action at the end of Acts.

3:21, 24 OT prophecy has a present, spiritual fulfillment in the church (v. 24) *and* a future fulfillment in the Second Coming of Christ. Bible prophecy is both realized and unfulfilled. The

PRAYING THE WORD

Lord, I pray for those in need of repentance and conversion, that their sins may be erased so that times of refreshing may come to them from Your presence.

Adapted from Acts 3:19

until the times of *b*restoration of all things, *c*which God has spoken by the mouth of all His holy prophets since *¹*the world began. 22For Moses truly said to the fathers, *a*"The LORD your God will raise up for you a Prophet like me from your brethren. Him you shall hear in all things, whatever He says to you. 23And it shall be *that* every soul who will not hear that Prophet shall be utterly destroyed from among the people.' 24Yes, and *a*all the prophets, from Samuel and those who follow, as many as have spoken, have also *¹*foretold these days. 25*a*You are sons of the prophets, and of the *covenant which God made with our fathers, saying to Abraham, *b*'And in your seed all the families of the earth shall be blessed.' 26To you *a*first, God, having raised up His Servant Jesus, sent Him to *bless you, *b*in turning away every one *of you* from your iniquities."

Peter and John Arrested

4 Now as they spoke to the people, the priests, the captain of the temple, and the *a*Sadducees came upon them, 2being greatly disturbed that they taught the people and preached in Jesus the resurrection from the dead. 3And they laid hands on them, and put *them* in custody until the next day, for it was already evening. 4However, many of those who heard the *word believed; and the number of the men came to be about five thousand.

Cross references (center column):

21 *b*Matt. 17:11; [Rom. 8:21]; *c*Luke 1:70 *¹*Or *time*
22 *a*Deut. 18:15, 18, 19; Acts 7:37
24 *a*2 Sam. 7:12; Luke 24:25 *¹*NU, M *proclaimed*
25 *a*Acts 2:39; [Rom. 9:4, 8; Gal. 3:26]; *b*Gen. 12:3; 18:18; 22:18; 26:4; 28:14 *See WW at Mark 14:24.
26 *a*Matt. 15:24; John 4:22; Acts 13:46; [Rom. 1:16; 2:9] *b*Is. 42:1; Matt. 1:21 *See WW at Luke 6:28.

CHAPTER 4
1 *a*Matt. 22:23
4 *See WW at Acts 19:20.

6 *a*Luke 3:2; John 11:49; 18:13
7 *a*Ex. 2:14; Matt. 21:23; Acts 7:27
8 *a*Luke 12:11, 12
10 *a*Acts 2:22; 3:6, 16 *b*Acts 2:24
11 *a*Ps. 118:22; Is. 28:16; Matt. 21:42
12 *a*Is. 42:1, 6, 7; 53:11; Dan. 9:24; [Matt. 1:21; John 14:6; Acts 10:43; 1 Tim. 2:5, 6] *See WW at Luke 19:9.
13 *a*Matt. 11:25; [1 Cor. 1:27] *See WW at John 1:5.
14 *a*Acts 3:11 *See WW at Matt. 12:22.
16 *a*John 11:47 *¹*remarkable *sign*

Addressing the Sanhedrin

5And it came to pass, on the next day, that their rulers, elders, and scribes, 6as well as *a*Annas the high priest, Caiaphas, John, and Alexander, and as many as were of the family of the high priest, were gathered together at Jerusalem. 7And when they had set them in the midst, they asked, *a*"By what power or by what name have you done this?"

8*a*Then Peter, filled with the Holy Spirit, said to them, "Rulers of the people and elders of Israel: 9If we this day are judged for a good deed *done* to a helpless man, by what means he has been made well, 10let it be known to you all, and to all the people of Israel, *a*that by the name of Jesus Christ of Nazareth, whom you crucified, *b*whom God raised from the dead, by Him this man stands here before you whole. 11This is the *a*'stone which was rejected by you builders, which has become the chief cornerstone.' 12*a*Nor is there *salvation in any other, for ① there is no **other** name under heaven given among men by which we must be saved."

The Name of Jesus Forbidden

13Now when they saw the boldness of ② Peter and John, *a*and *perceived that they were uneducated and untrained men, they marveled. And they realized that they had been with Jesus. 14And seeing the man who had been *healed *a*standing with them, they could say nothing against it. 15But when they had commanded them to go aside out of the council, they conferred among themselves, 16saying, *a*"What shall we do to these men? For, indeed, that a *¹*notable miracle

---

WORD WEALTH

4:12 other, *heteros;* Strong's #2087: Different, generic distinction, another kind, not of the same nature, form, or class. Here *heteros* denotes a distinction and an exclusivity, with no second choices, opinions, or options. "Jesus, You are the One. You are the only One. There is no *heteros*, no other!"

Bottom notes:

kingdom of God is both "now" and "later." **Whom heaven must receive:** See Ps. 110:1.

3:25 Peter reminds the Jewish leaders that the Abrahamic covenant promise of Gen. 12:1–3 shows that God never intended to limit His covenant blessing to the Jewish bloodline of Abraham's family.

4:1 The captain was the commander of the temple police, who were responsible to maintain public order in the temple precincts. **Sadducees:** See note on Matt. 16:6.

4:4 Men suggests that there may have been many women and children who were not counted in this early census (see 5:14).

4:5, 6 This gathering of officials was called the Sanhedrin, a kind of Jewish religious senate and supreme court.

4:8 See section 2 of Truth in Action at the end of Acts.

4:8 A believer's interaction with the Spirit is never static; therefore, Luke describes Peter's dynamic, ongoing relationship of the Spirit's power and anointing with the same words he used to describe his initial experience, being **filled with the Holy Spirit.** See notes on 2:4 and Eph. 5:18.

4:12 See section 1 of Truth in Action at the end of Acts.

4:13 See section 2 of Truth in Action at the end of Acts.

4:13 Uneducated means that the disciples had not received formal instruction in the rabbinical schools. **Untrained** describes them as common laymen, not professional experts.

4:16 The early debate over the Resurrection and other miracles concerned not whether such things occurred, but the meaning of the events.

has been done through them *is* [b]evident[2] to all who dwell in Jerusalem, and we cannot deny it. [17]But so that it spreads no further among the people, let us severely threaten them, that from now on they speak to no man in this name."

[18][a]So they called them and commanded them not to speak at all nor teach in the name of Jesus. [19]But Peter and John answered and said to them, [a]"Whether it is right in the sight of God to listen to you more than to God, you judge. [20][a]For we *cannot but speak the things which [b]we have seen and heard." [21]So when they had further threatened them, they let them go, finding no way of punishing them, [a]because of the people, since they all [b]glorified God for [c]what had been done. [22]For the man was over forty years old on whom this miracle of *healing had been performed.

Prayer for Boldness

[23]And being let go, [a]they went to their own *companions* and reported all that the chief priests and elders had said to them. [24]So when they heard that, they raised their voice to God *with one accord and said: *[a]"Lord, [a]You *are* God, who made heaven and earth and the sea, and all that is in them, [25]who [1]by the mouth of Your servant David have said:

[a]'Why did the nations rage,
And the people plot vain things?
26 The kings of the earth took their stand,
And the rulers were gathered together
Against the Lord and against His
Christ.'

KINGDOM DYNAMICS

4:24 One Voice, POWER OF UNITY. The third and fourth chapters of Acts relate the story of the first major crisis faced by the early church. Peter and John were imprisoned and then warned by the Jewish leaders to never again mention the name of Jesus. Instead of fleeing for their lives or separating from their brothers and sisters, they went immediately to the church and "reported all that the chief priests and elders had said to them" (v. 23). The members of the body of Christ responded together by raising their voices to God in prayer "with one accord." This is a vivid example of the kind of spiritual unity that results in the lives of those who are "filled with the Holy Spirit" and who "walk in the Spirit." (Acts 2:42/Acts 4:32, 33) P.A.C.

[27]"For [a]truly against [b]Your holy Servant Jesus, [c]whom You anointed, both Herod and Pontius Pilate, with the Gentiles and the people of Israel, were gathered together [28][a]to do whatever Your hand and Your purpose determined before to be done. [29]Now, Lord, look on their threats, and grant to Your servants [a]that with all boldness they may speak Your word, [30]by stretching out Your hand to *heal, [a]and that signs and wonders may be done [b]through the name of [c]Your holy Servant Jesus."

[31]And when they had prayed, [a]the place where they were assembled together was

WORD   WEALTH

4:31 boldness, *parrhēsia;* Strong's #3954: Outspokenness, unreserved utterance, freedom of speech, with frankness, candor, cheerful courage, and the opposite of cowardice, timidity, or fear. Here it denotes a divine enablement that comes to ordinary and unprofessional people exhibiting spiritual power and authority. It also refers to a clear presentation of the gospel without being ambiguous or unintelligible. *Parrhēsia* is not a human quality but a result of being filled with the Holy Spirit.

KINGDOM DYNAMICS

4:32, 33 One Heart and One Soul, POWER OF UNITY. The early church grew rapidly as "the Lord added to the church daily those who were being saved" (2:47). In 4:32, 33, it is reported that the growing multitude of believers were experiencing a profound dimension of spiritual unity. First, they were "of one heart," which is a description in the original Greek, meaning "in tune" or "in sync" with one another. To put it another way, they were all going the same way, spiritually together. Second, they were of "one soul" (sometimes translated as "one mind"). This has a wonderfully deep meaning in the original Greek. It literally means "to breathe" or "to breathe spiritually together." The results of this quality of spiritual unity were both powerful and practical: "they had all things in common" (shared everything they had); they witnessed "with great power"; and "great grace was upon them all." All of these glorious things took place through the unleashing of the power of the Holy Spirit in response to the corporate prayers of God's people crying out to Him together (v. 24). (Acts 4:24/Eph. 4:3–6) P.A.C.

Cross-references (center column):

16 [b]Acts 3:7–10
[2]*well known*
18 [a]Acts 5:28, 40
19 [a]Acts 5:29
20 [a]Acts 1:8; 2:32 [b]Acts 22:15; [1 John 1:1, 3]
*See WW at Jude 24.
21 [a]Matt. 21:26; Luke 20:6, 19; 22:2; Acts 5:26 [b]Matt. 15:31 [c]Acts 3:7, 8
22 *See WW at Luke 13:32.
23 [a]Acts 2:44–46; 12:12
24 [a]Ex. 20:11; 2 Kin. 19:15; Neh. 9:6; Ps. 146:6
*See WW at Acts 2:1. • See WW at Jude 4.
25 [a]Ps. 2:1, 2 [1]NU *through the Holy Spirit, by the mouth of our father, Your servant David,*

27 [a]Matt. 26:3; Luke 22:2; 23:1, 8 [b][Luke 1:35] [c]Luke 4:18; John 10:36
28 [a]Acts 2:23; 3:18
29 [a]Acts 4:13, 31; 9:27; 13:46; 14:3; 19:8; 26:26; Eph. 6:19
30 [a]Acts 2:43; 5:12 [b]Acts 3:6, 16 [c]Acts 4:27
*See WW at Luke 13:32.
31 [a]Matt. 5:6; Acts 2:2, 4; 16:26

4:19, 20 The superseding of obedience to God, in instances where human authority resists His will, is modeled in this passage. While it is apparently justifiable in some instances (see 5:40–42; 1 Pet. 2:18–23), there are no grounds in this text for the toleration of a rebellious spirit. Peter and John's demeanor, while asserting a higher moral claim, does not manifest either arrogance or presumption.

4:31 See note on 4:8.

shaken; and they were all filled with the Holy Spirit, [b]and they spoke the word of God with **boldness.**

Sharing in All Things

32Now the multitude of those who believed [a]were of one *heart and one soul;

WORD | WEALTH

4:33 power, *dunamis;* Strong's #1411: One of four great power words. The others are *exousia,* delegated authority; *ischuros,* great strength (esp. physical); and *kratos,* dominion authority. *Dunamis* means energy, power, might, great force, great ability, strength. It is sometimes used to describe the powers of the world to come at work upon the earth and divine power overcoming all resistance. (Cf. "dynamic," "dynamite," and "dynamometer.") The *dunamis* in Jesus resulted in dramatic transformations. This is the norm for the Spirit-filled and Spirit-led church.

KINGDOM | DYNAMICS

4:36 The Uplifting Demeanor of an Encourager (Barnabas), BIBLICAL MEN. Though his birth name was Joseph, the apostles called him Barnabas, which means: "Son of Encouragement" (4:36), a designation given to him that likely reflected his character. Throughout the Book of Acts Barnabas's encouraging spirit is on display through his actions and assignments: He was the first leader to embrace Saul (soon to be known as Paul) who he introduced to the apostles (9:27). The Jerusalem elders sent Barnabas to Antioch where he encouraged the Gentile disciples (11:22–26), before finding Paul and sponsoring him through ministry partnership in Antioch. After the Antioch church sent Barnabas and Saul to Jerusalem with a gift to encourage the believers there (11:27–30), they sent them out on a very effective missionary journey. As they prepared to launch into their second mission, Paul and Barnabas sharply disagreed about including John Mark, who had abandoned them early on their previous trip. Barnabas was compelled to bring John Mark with him (15:36, 37) and sponsored his restoration in ministry even though it meant separation from Paul. Believers can draw from the life of Barnabas in being a source of selfless, godly encouragement and sponsorship to other disciples who will go on to impact the world for the kingdom of God. (Dan. 6:3/Rom. 1:1). T.C./J.F

31 [b]Acts 4:29
32 [a]Acts 5:12;
Rom. 15:5, 6;
2 Cor. 13:11;
Phil. 1:27; 2:2;
1 Pet. 3:8
*See WW at Rev. 2:23.

[b]Acts 2:44
33 [a][Acts 1:8]
[b]Acts 1:22
[c]Rom. 6:15
*See WW at Rev. 15:5. • See WW at Acts 23:6.
34 [a][Matt. 19:21]; Acts 2:45
35 [a]Acts 4:37; 5:2 [b]Acts 2:45; 6:1
36 [1]NU *Joseph* [2]Or *Consolation*
37 [a]Acts 4:34, 35; 5:1, 2

CHAPTER 5
3 [a]Num. 30:2; Deut. 23:21; Eccl. 5:4 [b]Matt. 4:10; Luke 22:3; John 13:2, 27
5 [a]Ezek. 11:13; Acts 5:10, 11
6 [a]John 19:40
9 [a]Matt. 4:7; Acts 5:3, 4
*See WW at Matt. 18:19.
10 [a]Ezek. 11:13; Acts 5:5
11 [a]Acts 2:43; 5:5; 19:17

[b]neither did anyone say that any of the things he possessed was his own, but they had all things in common. 33And with [a]great **power** the apostles gave [b]witness* to the *resurrection of the Lord Jesus. And [c]great grace was upon them all. 34Nor was there anyone among them who lacked; [a]for all who were possessors of lands or houses sold them, and brought the proceeds of the things that were sold, 35[a]and laid *them* at the apostles' feet; [b]and they distributed to each as anyone had need.

36And [1]Joses, who was also named Barnabas by the apostles (which is translated Son of [2]Encouragement), a Levite of the country of Cyprus, 37[a]having land, sold *it,* and brought the money and laid *it* at the apostles' feet.

Lying to the Holy Spirit

5 But a certain man named Ananias, with Sapphira his wife, sold a possession. 2And he kept back *part* of the proceeds, his wife also being aware *of it,* and brought a certain part and laid *it* at the apostles' feet. 3[a]But Peter said, "Ananias, why has [b]Satan filled your heart to lie to the Holy Spirit and keep back *part* of the price of the land for yourself? 4While it remained, was it not your own? And after it was sold, was it not in your own control? Why have you conceived this thing in your heart? You have not lied to men but to God."

5Then Ananias, hearing these words, [a]fell down and breathed his last. So great fear came upon all those who heard these things. 6And the young men arose and [a]wrapped him up, carried *him* out, and buried *him.*

7Now it was about three hours later when his wife came in, not knowing what had happened. 8And Peter answered her, "Tell me whether you sold the land for so much?"

She said, "Yes, for so much."

9Then Peter said to her, "How is it that you have *agreed together [a]to test the Spirit of the Lord? Look, the feet of those who have buried your husband *are* at the door, and they will carry you out." 10[a]Then immediately she fell down at his feet and breathed her last. And the young men came in and found her dead, and carrying *her* out, buried *her* by her husband. 11[a]So great fear came upon all the church and upon all who heard these things.

5:1–11 Ananias and **Sapphira** were judged for their hypocrisy and lying to God, not for their decision to retain some of their personal property for themselves (v. 4). The severity of the punishment for such a small offense may seem intolerant and graceless (see Luke 9:54, 55), but it was necessary both to establish apostolic authority in the early church and to safeguard the church's purity. A sobering lesson is that Satan has the power to distort the thinking of Christians (Acts 5:3), thus affirming our need to allow him no place (Eph. 4:27). The believer's best defense against self-deception is through mutual accountability to other believers (especially to a local congregation, Eph. 5:21). Constant renewing of the mind through the Word and a sustained "fullness" of the Holy Spirit are also safeguards. See Rom. 12:1, 2; 2 Cor. 10:4, 5; Eph. 5:17–20.

WORD · WEALTH

5:13 esteemed, *megalunō;* Strong's #3170: To make great, to enlarge, to magnify, to increase, to make conspicuous, to extol, to show respect, to hold in high esteem. When Ananias and Sapphira were judged, many shrank from associating with the apostles and their services. Despite all this, the public looked at the new Christian worshipers favorably (*megalunō*).

Continuing Power in the Church

12And [a]through the hands of the apostles many signs and wonders were done among the people. [b]And they were all *with one accord in Solomon's Porch. 13Yet [a]none of the rest dared join them, [b]but the people **esteemed** them highly. 14And believers were increasingly added to the Lord, multitudes of both men and women, 15so that they brought the sick out into the streets and laid *them* on beds and couches, [a]that at least the shadow of Peter passing by might fall on some of them. 16Also a multitude gathered from the surrounding cities to Jerusalem, bringing [a]sick people and those who were tormented by unclean spirits, and they were all healed.

Imprisoned Apostles Freed

17[a]Then the high priest rose up, and all those who *were* with him (which is the *sect of the Sadducees), and they were filled with [l]indignation, 18[a]and laid their hands on the apostles and put them in the common prison. 19But at night [a]an angel of the Lord opened the prison doors and brought them out, and said, 20"Go, stand in the temple and speak to the people [a]all the words of this life."

21And when they heard *that,* they entered the temple early in the morning and taught. [a]But the high priest and those with him came and called the [l]council together, with all the [2]elders of the children of Israel, and sent to the prison to have them brought.

Apostles on Trial Again

22But when the officers came and did not find them in the prison, they returned and reported, 23saying, "Indeed we found the prison shut securely, and the guards standing [l]outside before the doors; but

---

12 [a]Acts 2:43;
4:30; 6:8; 14:3;
15:12; [Rom.
15:19]; 2 Cor.
12:12; Heb. 2:4
[b]Acts 3:11;
4:32
*See WW at
Acts 2:1.
13 [a]John 9:22
[b]Acts 2:47;
4:21
15 [a]Matt. 9:21;
14:36; Acts
19:12
16 [a]Mark 16:17,
18; [John
14:12]
17 [a]Matt. 3:7;
Acts 4:1, 2, 6
[l]jealousy
*See WW at
2 Pet. 2:1.
18 [a]Luke 21:12;
Acts 4:3;
16:37
19 [a]Matt. 1:20,
24; 2:13, 19;
28:2; Luke
1:11; 2:9; Acts
12:7; 16:26
20 [a][John 6:63,
68; 17:3;
1 John 5:11]
21 [a]Acts 4:5, 6
[l]Sanhedrin
[2]council of
elders or
senate
23 [l]NU, M omit
outside

24 [a]Luke 22:4;
Acts 4:1; 5:26
[l]NU omits the
high priest
25 [l]NU, M omit
saying
26 [a]Matt. 21:26
28 [a]Acts 4:17,
18 [b]Acts 2:23,
36 [c]Matt.
23:35
*See WW at Acts
16:24.
29 [a]Acts 4:19
30 [a]Acts 3:13,
15 [b]Acts 10:39;
13:29; [Gal.
3:13; 1 Pet.
2:24]
31 [a]Mark 16:19;
[Acts 2:33, 36;
Phil. 2:9–11]
[b]Acts 3:15;
Rev. 1:5 [c]Matt.
1:21 [d]Luke
24:47; [Eph.
1:7; Col. 1:14]
*See WW at
James 4:10. ·
See WW at
Heb. 9:22.
32 [a]John 15:26,
27; Acts 15:28;
Rom. 8:16;
Heb. 2:4 [b]Acts
2:4; 10:44
33 [a]Acts 2:37;
7:54 [l]cut to the
quick

KINGDOM · DYNAMICS

5:19 Angels in the NT, ANGELS. There are more direct references to angels in the NT than in the OT. Jesus talked about angels (Matt. 26:53; Mark 13:32; Luke 20:34–36; John 1:51); and not only were angels in attendance at His birth, resurrection, and ascension, they were active amid the early church's life. In Acts, angelic activity: (1) freed apostles imprisoned for their faith (see also 12:6, 7), (2) led Philip to an evangelistic opportunity (8:26), (3) told Cornelius how to find Peter in order to hear the gospel (10:3, 5), (4) struck judgment on wicked Herod (12:23), and (5) encouraged Paul caught in a killer storm (27:23). Throughout the NT, believers are given instruction on the presence, nature, and function of angels, fallen and unfallen (Heb. 1:14; 1 Pet. 1:12; 3:22; Rev. 5:11, 12; Eph. 6:12; Col. 1:16; 2 Pet. 2:4). (Is. 14:12–14/Rev. 1:1) B.C.

---

when we opened them, we found no one inside!" 24Now when [l]the high priest, [a]the captain of the temple, and the chief priests heard these things, they wondered what the outcome would be. 25So one came and told them, [l]saying, "Look, the men whom you put in prison are standing in the temple and teaching the people!"

26Then the captain went with the officers and brought them without violence, [a]for they feared the people, lest they should be stoned. 27And when they had brought them, they set *them* before the council. And the high priest asked them, 28saying, [a]"Did we not strictly *command you not to teach in this name? And look, you have filled Jerusalem with your doctrine, [b]and intend to bring this Man's [c]blood on us!"

29But Peter and the *other* apostles answered and said: [a]"We ought to obey God rather than men. 30[a]The God of our fathers raised up Jesus whom you murdered by [b]hanging on a tree. 31[a]Him God has *exalted to His right hand *to be* [b]Prince and [c]Savior, [d]to give repentance to Israel and *forgiveness of sins. 32And [a]we are His witnesses to these things, and *so also is* the Holy Spirit [b]whom God has given to those who obey Him."

Gamaliel's Advice

33When they heard *this,* they were [a]furious[l] and plotted to kill them. 34Then one in the council stood up, a Pharisee named

---

5:12 Signs and wonders characterized the ministry of the early church and are equally intended to be expected in and through the church today. See text and notes on 1 Cor. 12:1–31.

5:15 The shadow of Peter was not magic nor was it intended to provide a formula. Sometimes God uses physical objects as a point at which our faith may make a kind of link between the seen and the unseen (see 19:12). The bread and cup of Communion, the water of baptism, and the anointing oil (James 5:14) are some examples.

5:31, 32 The gift of the Holy Spirit, whom Luke notes is given to all believers at the time of salvation, bears witness to the reality of the exaltation of Jesus (see 2:33; John 7:39).

[a]Gamaliel, a teacher of the law held in respect by all the people, and commanded them to put the apostles outside for a little while. [35]And he said to them: "Men of Israel, [l]take heed to yourselves what you intend to do regarding these men. [36]For some time ago Theudas rose up, claiming to be somebody. A number of men, about four hundred, [l]joined* him. He was slain, and all who obeyed him were scattered and came to nothing. [37]After this man, Judas of Galilee rose up in the days of the census, and drew away many people after him. He also perished, and all who obeyed him were dispersed. [38]And now I say to you, keep away from these men and let them alone; for if this plan or this work is of men, it will come to nothing; [39][a]but if it is of God, you cannot overthrow it—lest you even be found [b]to fight against God."

[40]And they agreed with him, and when they had [a]called for the apostles [b]and beaten *them,* they commanded that they should not speak in the name of Jesus, and let them go. [41]So they departed from the presence of the council, [a]rejoicing that they were counted *worthy to suffer shame for [l]His name. [42]And daily [a]in the temple, and in every house, [b]they did not cease teaching and preaching Jesus *as* the Christ.

Seven Chosen to Serve

(3) **6** Now in those days, [a]when *the number of* the *disciples was multiplying, there arose a complaint against the Hebrews by the [b]Hellenists,[l] because their widows were neglected [c]in the daily distribution. [2]Then the twelve summoned the multitude of the disciples and said, [a]"It is not desirable that we should leave the word of God and serve tables. [3]Therefore, brethren, [a]seek out from among you seven men of *good* reputation, full of the Holy Spirit

---

Cross references column:

34 [a]Acts 22:3
35 [l]be careful
36 [l]followed
*See WW at Mark 10:7.
39 [a]Luke 21:15; 1 Cor. 1:25 [b]Acts 7:51; 9:5
40 [a]Acts 4:18 [b]Matt. 10:17; Mark 13:9; Acts 16:22, 23; 21:32; 2 Cor. 11:25
41 [a]Matt. 5:10–12; Rom. 5:3; 2 Cor. 12:10; Heb. 10:34; [James 1:2; 1 Pet. 4:13–16] [l]NU *the name;* M *the name of Jesus*
*See WW at 2 Thess. 1:5.
42 [a]Acts 2:46 [b]Acts 4:20, 29

CHAPTER 6
1 [a]Acts 2:41; 4:4 [b]Acts 9:29; 11:20 [c]Acts 4:35; 11:29 [l]Greek-speaking Jews
*See WW at Matt. 10:1.
2 [a]Ex. 18:17
3 [a]Deut. 1:13; 1 Tim. 3:7

[b]Phil. 1:1; 1 Tim. 3:8–13
4 [a]Acts 2:42
5 [a]Acts 6:3; 11:24 [b]Acts 8:5, 26; 21:8 [c]Rev. 2:6, 15
6 [a]Acts 1:24 [b]Num. 8:10; 27:18; Deut. 34:9; [Mark 5:23; Acts 8:17; 9:17; 13:3; 19:6; 1 Tim. 4:14; 2 Tim. 1:6]; Heb. 6:2
7 [a]Acts 12:24; Col. 1:6 [b]John 12:42
*See WW at Rom. 6:17.
8 [a]Acts 2:43; 5:12; 8:15; 14:3 [l]NU *grace*

---

and wisdom, whom we may appoint over this [b]business; [4]but we [a]will give ourselves continually to prayer and to the ministry of the word."

[5]And the saying pleased the whole multitude. And they chose Stephen, [a]a man full of faith and the Holy Spirit, and [b]Philip, Prochorus, Nicanor, Timon, Parmenas, and [c]Nicolas, a proselyte from Antioch, [6]whom they set before the apostles; and [a]when they had prayed, [b]they laid hands on them.

[7]Then [a]the word of God spread, and the number of the disciples multiplied greatly in Jerusalem, and a great many [b]of the priests were *obedient to the faith.

Stephen Accused of Blasphemy

[8]And Stephen, full of [l]faith and power, did great [a]wonders and signs among the

---

5:33–40 Gamaliel, Paul's former **teacher** (22:3), did not see Jesus as the Messiah, but his counsel to the Sanhedrin was certainly influenced by divine providence. Luke's more subtle message is that even the highest levels of Jewish leadership had to admit that they had no valid reason for resisting the early church.

5:41 Rejoicing that they were counted worthy to suffer shame for His name is a response that would be unusual for some Christians today. Jesus does not guarantee perpetual happiness if we agree to serve Him, but He does promise us a joy that is "inexpressible and full of glory" (1 Pet. 1:8).

5:42 Both public services in the temple and small group meetings in private homes were served the purpose of nurturing the believers. Luke establishes both types of meetings as a paradigm, vital to the life of any local congregation (see 2:46).

6:1–6 See section 3 of Truth in Action at the end of Acts.

6:1 The Hebrews were natives of Israel and spoke Hebrew (or Aramaic) rather than Greek. **The Hellenists** were Jews who were natives of the Greco-Roman world and spoke Greek. The presence and power of the Spirit does not automatically guarantee that

life's difficulties will go away. Often it is necessary for Christians to discuss their differences and ask God for wise solutions.

6:3 Church growth demands organization and delegation. Leadership in the church must be full of *both* **the Holy Spirit and wisdom.** The Holy Spirit gives us God's perspective. Wisdom is the practical side of problem solving. Many interpreters regard the **seven** as the first deacons, although the term does not appear in this passage.

6:4 Prayer and **the ministry of the word** must be the perpetual priority of the equipping leadership of the church (see Eph. 4:11–16). This does not suggest that the ministry of benevolence is on a lower level. It is a matter of the roles that God assigns (see Rom. 12:4–8).

6:6 Laid hands on them is an act of ordination, a transferring of authority and responsibility, also indicating an acknowledgment of mutual identification and partnership with those commissioned to service.

6:7 This is the first of six progress reports that appear throughout Acts (v. 7; 9:31; 12:24; 16:5; 19:20; 28:31). Each covers an approximate span of five years.

6:8 Wonders and signs are not an exclusive characteristic of

WORD WEALTH

6:10 wisdom, *sophia;* Strong's #4678: Practical wisdom, prudence, skill, comprehensive insight, Christian enlightenment, a right application of knowledge, insight into the true nature of things. Wisdom in the Bible is often coupled with knowledge (Rom. 11:33; 1 Cor. 12:8; Col. 2:3). In anticipation of our needing guidance, direction, and knowing, God tells us to ask for wisdom, assuring us of a liberal reception (James 1:5).

WORD WEALTH

6:11 blasphemous, *blasphēmos;* Strong's #989: Compare "blasphemy." From *blaptō*, "to injure," and *phēme*, "speech"; hence, slanderous, abusive speech.

people. 9Then there arose some from what is called the Synagogue of the Freedmen (Cyrenians, Alexandrians, and those from Cilicia and Asia), disputing with Stephen. 10And *a*they were not able to *resist the **wisdom** and the Spirit by which he spoke. 11*a*Then they secretly induced men to say, "We have heard him speak **blasphemous** words against Moses and God." 12And they stirred up the people, the elders, and the scribes; and they came upon *him,* seized him, and brought *him* to the council. 13They also set up false witnesses who said, "This man does not cease to speak *l*blasphemous* words against this holy place and the law; 14*a*for we have heard him say that this Jesus of Nazareth will destroy this place and change the customs which Moses delivered to us." 15And all who sat in the council, looking steadfastly at him, saw his face as the face of an angel.

Stephen's Address: The Call of Abraham

7 Then the high priest said, "Are these things so?"

2And he said, *a*"Brethren and fathers, listen: The *b*God of *glory appeared to our father Abraham when he was in Mesopota-

---

10 *a*Ex. 4:12; Is. 54:17; Luke 21:15
*See WW at Eph. 6:13.
11 *a*1 Kin. 21:10, 13; Matt. 26:59, 60
13 *l*NU omits *blasphemous*
*See WW at Acts 6:11.
14 *a*Acts 10:38; 25:8

CHAPTER 7
2 *a*Acts 22:1
*b*Ps. 29:3;
1 Cor. 2:8
*See WW at John 2:11.

*c*Gen. 11:31, 32
3 *a*Gen. 12:1
4 *a*Gen. 11:31;
15:7; Heb.
11:8–10 *b*Gen. 11:32
5 *a*Gen. 12:7;
13:15; 15:3, 18; 17:8; 26:3
*See WW at Matt. 27:19.
6 *a*Gen. 15:13, 14, 16; 47:11, 12 *b*Ex. 1:8–14; 12:40, 41; Gal. 3:17
*See WW at Eph. 2:19.
7 *a*Gen. 15:14 *b*Ex. 14:13–31 *c*Ex. 3:12; Josh. 3:1–17
8 *a*Gen. 17:9–14 *b*Gen. 21:1–5 *c*Gen. 25:21–26 *d*Gen. 29:31–30:24; 35:18, 22–26
9 *a*Gen. 37:4, 11, 28; Ps. 105:17 *b*Gen. 37:28 *c*Gen. 39:2, 21, 23
*See WW at 1 Cor. 14:1.
10 *a*Gen. 41:38–44
*See WW at Acts 6:10.
11 *a*Gen. 41:54; 42:5 *l*affliction
12 *a*Gen. 42:1, 2

WORD WEALTH

7:5 promised, *epaggellō;* Strong's #1861: To engage, to profess, to assert something concerning oneself, to announce what one is about to do (an intention), to render a service, to make a commitment, to pledge to do something. Here *epaggellō* is God's assurance to Abraham that the land He showed him was for him and his descendants.

mia, before he dwelt in *c*Haran, 3and said to him, *a*'Get out of your country and from your relatives, and come to a land that I will show you.' 4Then *a*he came out of the land of the Chaldeans and dwelt in Haran. And from there, when his father was *b*dead, He moved him to this land in which you now dwell. 5And *God* gave him no inheritance in it, not even *enough* to *set his foot on. But even when *Abraham* had no child, *a*He **promised** to give it to him for a possession, and to his descendants after him. 6But God spoke in this way: *a*that his descendants would *dwell in a foreign land, and that they would bring them into *b*bondage and oppress *them* four hundred years. 7*a*'And the nation to whom they will be in bondage I will *b*judge,' said God, *c*'and after that they shall come out and serve Me in this place.' 8*a*Then He gave him the covenant of circumcision; *b*and so *Abraham* begot Isaac and circumcised him on the eighth day; *c*and Isaac *begot* Jacob, and *d*Jacob *begot* the twelve patriarchs.

The Patriarchs in Egypt

9*a*"And the patriarchs, becoming *envious, *b*sold Joseph into Egypt. *c*But God was with him 10and delivered him out of all his troubles, *a*and gave him favor and *wisdom in the presence of Pharaoh, king of Egypt; and he made him governor over Egypt and all his house. 11*a*Now a famine and great *l*trouble came over all the land of Egypt and Canaan, and our fathers found no sustenance. 12*a*But when Jacob heard that there was grain in Egypt, he sent out our fathers first. 13And the

---

apostolic ministry. **Stephen** was not an apostle, but he was **full of faith and power.**

6:9 Freedmen were former Roman slaves.

6:10 Testifying of your faith is not just a matter of saying the right things. Witnessing is a spiritual battle that requires **the wisdom** and the power of the **Spirit** working in the witness.

6:13, 14 The same argument had been leveled at Jesus (Matt. 26:60, 61). Actually, the coming of Christ meant the end of the temple order, which was the foundation and centerpiece of Judaism.

7:1–53 Stephen's lengthy address is more than a rebuttal of the

charges against him. Rather than defending himself, he brought an indictment against his accusers. Instead of manifesting a true zeal for the temple and the Law in their opposition to the gospel, the Jews were displaying the same rebellious spirit of unbelief that characterized their forebears who resisted the purposes of God. In a skillful review of Israel's history, he also concludes that God's presence is not limited to a geographical place nor to a particular people.

7:8 The covenant of circumcision was intended to reflect personal commitment to one's obedience to God's covenant, but the Jews made little distinction between the ritual and the reality (see Rom. 4:9–12). **The twelve patriarchs** are the sons of Jacob, who became the fathers of the 12 tribes of Israel.

*a*second *time* Joseph was made known to his brothers, and Joseph's family became known to the Pharaoh. 14*a*Then Joseph sent and called his father Jacob and *b*all his relatives to *him*, 1seventy-five people. 15*a*So Jacob went down to Egypt; *b*and he died, he and our fathers. 16And *a*they were carried back to Shechem and laid in *b*the tomb that Abraham bought for a sum of money from the sons of Hamor, *the father* of Shechem.

God Delivers Israel by Moses

17"But when *a*the time of the promise drew near which God had sworn to Abraham, *b*the people grew and multiplied in Egypt 18till another king *a*arose who did not know Joseph. 19This man dealt treacherously with our people, and oppressed our forefathers, *a*making them expose their babies, so that they might not live. 20*a*At this time Moses was born, and *b*was well pleasing to God; and he was brought up in his father's house for three months. 21But *a*when he was set out, *b*Pharaoh's daughter took him away and brought him up as her own son. 22And Moses was learned in all the wisdom of the Egyptians, and was *a*mighty in words and *deeds.

23*a*"Now when he was forty years old, it came into his heart to visit his brethren, the children of Israel. 24And seeing one of *them* suffer wrong, he defended and avenged him who was oppressed, and struck down the Egyptian. 25For he supposed that his brethren would have understood that God would deliver them by his hand, but they did not understand. 26And the next day he appeared to *two of* them as they were fighting, and *tried to* reconcile them, saying, 'Men, you are brethren; why *do you wrong one another?' 27But he who did his neighbor wrong pushed him away, saying, *a*'Who made you a ruler and a judge over us? 28Do you want to kill me as you did the Egyptian yesterday?' 29*a*Then, at this saying, Moses fled and became a *dweller in the land of Midian, where he *b*had two sons.

30*a*"And when forty years had passed, an Angel 1of the Lord appeared to him in a flame of fire in a bush, in the wilderness of Mount Sinai. 31When Moses saw *it*, he marveled at the sight; and as he drew near to observe, the voice of the Lord came to him, 32*saying*, *a*'I *am* the God of your fathers—the God of Abraham, the God of Isaac, and the God of Jacob.' And Moses trembled and dared not look. 33*a*Then the LORD said to him, "Take your sandals off your feet, for

---

13 *a*Gen. 45:4, 16
14 *a*Gen. 45:9, 27 *b*Gen. 46:26, 27; Deut. 10:22 1Or *seventy*, Ex. 1:5
15 *a*Gen. 46:1–7 *b*Gen. 49:33; Ex. 1:6
16 *a*Gen. 50:13; Ex. 13:19; Josh. 24:32 *b*Gen. 23:16
17 *a*Gen. 15:13; Ex. 2:23–25; Acts 7:6, 7 *b*Ex. 1:7–9; Ps. 105:24, 25
18 *a*Ex. 1:8
19 *a*Ex. 1:22 *b*Heb. 11:23
20 *a*Ex. 2:1, 2 *b*Heb. 11:23
21 *a*Ex. 2:3, 4 *b*Ex. 2:5–10
22 *a*Luke 24:19 *See WW at John 9:4.
23 *a*Ex. 2:11, 12; Heb. 11:24–26
26 *See WW at Acts 25:10.
27 *a*Ex. 2:14; Luke 12:14; Acts 7:35
29 *a*Heb. 11:27 *b*Ex. 2:15, 21, 22; 4:20; 18:3 *See WW at Eph. 2:19.
30 *a*Ex. 3:1–10; Is. 63:9 1NU omits *of the Lord*
32 *a*Ex. 3:6, 15; [Matt. 22:32]; Heb. 11:16
33 *a*Ex. 3:5, 7, 8, 10
34 *a*Ex. 2:24, 25 *b*Ps. 105:26
35 *a*Ex. 2:14; Acts 7:27 *b*Ex. 14:21
36 *a*Ex. 12:41; 33:1; Deut. 6:21, 23; Heb. 8:9 Rev. 7:8, 9; Deut. 6:22; Ps. 105:27; John 4:48 *c*Ex. 14:21 *d*Ex. 16:1, 35; Num. 14:33; Ps. 95:8–10; Acts 7:42; 13:18; Heb. 3:8 *See WW at Acts 15:12.
37 *a*Deut. 18:15, 18, 19; Acts 3:22 *b*Matt. 17:5 1NU, M omit *Him you shall hear*
38 *a*Ex. 19:3 *b*Is. 63:9; Gal. 3:19; Heb. 2:2 *c*Ex. 21:1; Deut. 5:27; John 1:17 *d*Rom. 3:2; Heb. 5:12; 1 Pet. 4:11 1Gr. *ekklesia*, assembly or church 2sayings
39 *a*Ps. 95:8–11
40 *a*Ex. 32:1, 23
41 *a*Ex. 32:2–4; Deut. 9:16; Ps. 106:19 *b*Ex. 32:6, 18, 19
42 *a*Ps. 81:12; [2 Thess. 2:11] *b*Deut. 4:19; 2 Kin. 21:3 *c*Amos 5:25–27
43 *a*2 Chr. 36:11–21; Jer. 25:9–12

---

the place where you stand is **holy** ground. 34I have surely *a*seen the oppression of My people who are in Egypt; I have heard their groaning and have come down to deliver them. And now come, I will *b*send you to Egypt." '

35"This Moses whom they rejected, saying, *a*'Who made you a ruler and a judge?' is the one God sent *to be* a ruler and a deliverer *b*by the hand of the Angel who appeared to him in the bush. 36*a*He brought them out, after he had *b*shown *wonders and signs in the land of Egypt, *c*and in the Red Sea, *d*and in the wilderness forty years.

Israel Rebels Against God

37"This is that Moses who said to the children of Israel, *a*'The LORD your God will raise up for you a Prophet like me from your brethren. *b*Him1 you shall hear.'

38*a*"This is he who was in the 1congregation in the wilderness with *b*the Angel who spoke to him on Mount Sinai, and *with* our fathers, *c*the one who received the living *d*oracles2 to give to us, 39whom our fathers *a*would not obey, but rejected. And in their hearts they turned back to Egypt, 40*a*saying to Aaron, 'Make us gods to go before us; *as for* this Moses who brought us out of the land of Egypt, we do not know what has become of him.' 41*a*And they made a calf in those days, offered sacrifices to the idol, and *b*rejoiced in the works of their own hands. 42Then *a*God turned and gave them up to worship *b*the host of heaven, as it is written in the book of the Prophets:

c'Did you offer Me slaughtered animals
and sacrifices *during* forty years in
the wilderness,
O house of Israel?
43 You also took up the tabernacle of
Moloch,
And the star of your god
Remphan,
Images which you made to worship;
And *a*I will carry you away beyond
Babylon.'

God's True Tabernacle

44"Our fathers had the tabernacle of *witness in the wilderness, as He appointed, instructing Moses [a]to make it according to the pattern that he had seen, 45[a]which our fathers, having received it in turn, also brought with Joshua into the land possessed by the Gentiles, [b]whom God drove out before the face of our fathers until the [c]days of David, 46[a]who found favor before God and [b]asked to find a dwelling for the God of Jacob. 47[a]But Solomon built Him a house.

48"However, [a]the Most High does not dwell in temples made with hands, as the prophet says:

49 'Heaven[a] is My throne,
And earth is My footstool.
What house will you build for Me? says the LORD,
Or what is the place of My rest?
50 Has My hand not [a]made all these things?'

Israel Resists the Holy Spirit

51"You [a]stiff-necked[1] and [b]uncircumcised in heart and ears! You always resist the Holy Spirit; as your fathers did, so do you. 52[a]Which of the prophets did your fathers not persecute? And they killed those who foretold the coming of [b]the Just One, of whom you now have become the betrayers and murderers, 53[a]who have received the law by the direction of *angels and have not kept it."

Stephen the Martyr

54[a]When they heard these things they were [1]cut to the heart, and they gnashed at him with their teeth. 55But he, [a]being full of the Holy Spirit, gazed into heaven and saw the [b]glory of God, and Jesus standing at the right hand of God, 56and said, "Look! [a]I *see the heavens opened and the [b]Son of Man standing at the right hand of God!"

57Then they cried out with a loud voice, *stopped their ears, and ran at him *with

one accord; 58and they cast him out of the city and stoned him. And [a]the *witnesses laid down their clothes at the feet of a young man named Saul. 59And they stoned Stephen as he was calling on God and saying, "Lord Jesus, [a]receive my spirit." 60Then he knelt down and cried out with a loud voice, [a]"Lord, do not charge them with this *sin." And when he had said this, he fell asleep.

Saul Persecutes the Church

8 Now Saul was consenting to his death. At that time a great **persecution** arose against the **church** which was at Jerusalem; and [a]they were all scattered throughout the regions of Judea and Samaria, except the apostles. 2And devout men carried Stephen to his burial, and [a]made great lamentation over him.

3As for Saul, [a]he made havoc of the church, entering every house, and dragging off men and women, committing them to prison.

Christ Is Preached in Samaria

4Therefore [a]those who were scattered went everywhere preaching the word. 5Then [a]Philip went down to [1]the city of Samaria

Cross-references (center column)

44 [a]Ex. 25:40; [Heb. 8:5]
*See WW at Rev. 15:5.
45 [a]Deut. 32:49; Josh. 3:14; 18:1; 23:9
[b]Neh. 9:24; Ps. 44:2 [c]2 Sam. 6:2–15
46 [a]2 Sam. 7:1–13; 1 Kin. 8:17 [b]1 Chr. 22:7; Ps. 132:4, 5
47 [a]1 Kin. 6:1–38; 8:20, 21; 2 Chr. 3:1–17
48 [a]1 Kin. 8:27; 2 Chr. 2:6; Acts 17:24
49 [a]Is. 66:1, 2; Matt. 5:34
50 [a]Ps. 102:25
51 [a]Ex. 32:9; Is. 6:10
[b]Lev. 26:41
[1]stubborn
52 [a]2 Chr. 36:16; Matt. 21:35; 23:35; 1 Thess. 2:15 [b]Acts 3:14; 22:14; 1 John 2:1
53 [a]Ex. 20:1; Deut. 33:2; Acts 7:38; Gal. 3:19; Heb. 2:2
*See WW at Matt. 4:11.
54 [a]Acts 5:33
[1]furious
55 [a]Matt. 5:8; 16:28; Mark 9:1; Luke 9:27; Acts 6:5 [b]Ex. 24:17]
56 [a]Matt. 3:16
[b]Dan. 7:13
*See WW at John 20:14.
57 *See WW at 2 Cor. 5:14. • See WW at Acts 2:1.
58 [a]Acts 22:20
*See WW at Rev. 1:5.
59 [a]Ps. 31:5
60 [a]Matt. 5:44; Luke 23:34
*See WW at John 1:29.
CHAPTER 8
1 [a]John 16:2; Acts 8:4; 11:19
2 [a]Gen. 23:2
3 [a]Acts 7:58; 1 Cor. 15:9; Gal. 1:13; Phil. 3:6; 1 Tim. 1:13
4 [a]Matt. 10:23
5 [a]Acts 6:5; 8:26, 30 [1]Or a

WORD | WEALTH

8:1 persecution, *diōgmos*; Strong's #1375: Persecution is the hatred and affliction that follows the witness and holy life of God's people in a hostile world. Jesus taught that God's prophets always faced persecution (Matt. 5:12), so His disciples should expect the same (Matt. 10:23). The early Christians saw the persecution of Jesus' followers as a participation in His redemptive suffering: filling up "what is lacking in the afflictions of Christ" (Col. 1:24). The idea of the coming Messiah held that the suffering of God's people was part of the coming of the kingdom—evidence that a person is truly one of God's own. Therefore they are "blessed" (Matt. 5:10) and should "rejoice" and "glorify God." The word is also used in 2 Thessalonians 1:4 and 2 Corinthians 12:10.

Footnotes (bottom)

7:44 Tabernacle of witness: The stone tablets of the Ten Commandments were referred to as "the witness," or "the Testimony," being contained within the ark of the covenant in the tabernacle of Moses.

7:47, 48 Stephen was not opposed to the temple itself, but to the lifeless institutionalism that came to represent.

7:51–53 Stephen's passionate conclusion led to his violent death. **Uncircumcised in heart and ears** describes those who felt self-assured because they had been outwardly circumcised. Ritualism does not bring one into a right standing before God. A change of heart through rebirth and an obedient walk of faith are the real signs of a true relationship with God.

7:55, 56 Son of Man: See Introduction to Matthew: Christ Revealed and note on Mark 2:9–12. Jesus, who sits at the right

hand of the Father (Col. 3:1; Heb. 1:3, 13; 10:12), is **standing** here to witness against Stephen's accusers and to receive him into the heavenly kingdom.

7:58 Saul, the one who will become the apostle Paul, was from Tarsus, located in Cilicia. He may have even attended the synagogue where Stephen preached (6:9).

7:60 Stephen's prayer is reminiscent of that of Jesus at His Crucifixion (Luke 23:34).

8:4 God works maturity and redemptive good in the midst of evil (see note on Rom. 8:28). The first official persecution of the church drove the Christians out of Jerusalem, and they preached the gospel everywhere they went.

8:5, 6 Philip, like Stephen, was not an apostle (6:8), but that was

WORD WEALTH

8:1 church, *ekklēsia;* Strong's #1577: Used in secular Greek for an assembly of citizens and in the Septuagint for the congregation of Israel. The NT uses the word in the former sense in 19:32, 39, 41, and in the latter sense in 7:38 and Hebrews 2:12. The dominant use in the NT is to describe an assembly or company of Christians in the following ways: (1) the whole body of Christians; (2) a local church constituting a company of Christians gathering for worship, sharing, and teaching; and (3) churches in a district. Other related terms are: "spiritual house," "chosen race," and "God's people." (Cf. "ecclesiastic" and "ecclesiastical.") The survival of the Christian church against all its opponents is assured in Jesus' words from Matthew 16:18, "On this rock I will build My church, and the gates of Hades shall not prevail against it."

and *preached Christ to them. 6And the multitudes *with one accord heeded the things spoken by Philip, hearing and seeing the miracles which he did. 7For ᵃunclean spirits, crying with a loud voice, came out of many who were possessed; and many who

were paralyzed and lame were healed. 8And there was great joy in that city.

The Sorcerer's Profession of Faith

9But there was a certain man called Simon, who previously ᵃpracticed ¹sorcery in the city and ᵇastonished the ²people of Samaria, claiming that he was someone great, 10to whom they all gave heed, from the least to the greatest, saying, "This man is the great power of God." 11And they heeded him because he had astonished them with his ¹sorceries for a long time. 12But when they believed Philip as he preached the things ᵃconcerning the kingdom of God and the name of Jesus Christ, both men and women were baptized. 13Then Simon himself also believed; and when he was baptized he continued with Philip, and was amazed, seeing the miracles and signs which were done.

The Sorcerer's Sin

14Now when the ᵃapostles who were at Jerusalem heard that Samaria had received the word of God, they sent Peter and John to them, 15who, when they had come down,

5 *See WW at Acts 9:20.
6 *See WW at Acts 2:1.
7 ᵃMark 16:17

9 ᵃActs 8:11; 13:6 ᵇActs 5:36 ¹*magic* ²*Or nation*
11 ¹*magic arts*
12 ᵃActs 1:3; 8:4
14 ᵃActs 5:12, 29, 40

no hindrance to his miracle ministry. Miracles themselves do not bring salvation, but they often attract people to the message. The miracles of the Bible are "signs," in that each one conveys an important spiritual message, as well as serving to confirm the veracity of the word of the gospel (Mark 16:20).

8:14 Since the Samaritans were the first non-Jews to receive the gospel, the Jerusalem church sent Peter and John to Samaria as an official, apostolic delegation to investigate (see John 4:9 for Jewish-Samaritan relationships). This was a direct fulfillment of Acts 1:8.

PHILIP'S MISSIONARY JOURNEYS

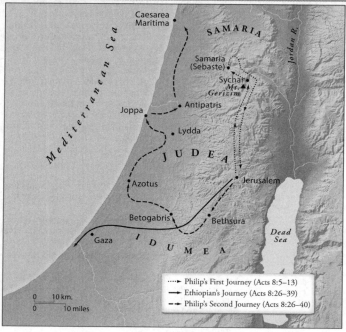

- ······▶ Philip's First Journey (Acts 8:5–13)
- ——▶ Ethiopian's Journey (Acts 8:26–39)
- – –▶ Philip's Second Journey (Acts 8:26–40)

◀ Two journeys are recorded in Acts 8:5–13 and 8:26–40.

15 ªActs 2:38;
19:2
16 ªActs 19:2
ᵇMatt. 28:19;
Acts 2:38
ᶜActs 10:48;
19:5
17 ªActs 6:6;
19:6; Heb. 6:2
20 ª2 Kin. 5:16;
Is. 55:1; Dan.
5:17; [Matt.
10:8] ᵇ[Acts
2:38; 10:45;
11:17]
21 ªJer. 17:9
22 ªDan. 4:27;
2 Tim. 2:25
23 ªHeb. 12:15
*See WW at
John 7:18.
24 ªGen. 20:7,
17; Ex. 8:8;
Num. 21:7;
1 Kin. 13:6;
Job 42:8;
James 5:16

26 ªActs 6:5
ˡOr a deserted
place
27 ªPs. 68:31;
87:4; Is. 56:3;
Zeph. 3:10
ᵇ1 Kin. 8:41,
42; John
12:20

KINGDOM DYNAMICS

8:14 A Spirit-Filled Revival, HOLY SPIRIT FULLNESS. Peter and John's concern for the Samaritan revival directly relates to their desire that those born of the Holy Spirit also receive the fullness of the Holy Spirit. The text and their ministry clearly differentiate water baptism (vv. 12, 16) from receiving the Holy Spirit's fullness (v. 17). The apostles laid hands on the converts, and they received the Holy Spirit with miracle signs. This attracted the interest of Simon the sorcerer (vv. 18, 19), who desired the same power demonstrated by the apostles as they laid hands on the converts. For the apostles, the Holy Spirit fullness was no small matter; their focus and approach were dedicated toward guaranteeing the transmission of the power of Pentecost among new believers. They obviously felt the need for every believer to become equipped with power, as sure as each of them had received new life in Christ and obeyed Him in water baptism. Such leadership is still needed in the church today. (Acts 2:4–13/Acts 9:17) S.G.B.

KINGDOM DYNAMICS

8:23 The Bonds of Unforgiveness, DELIVERANCE. A sorcerer is one who deceives, manipulates, and delights to control others and does so by demonic enablement. Peter identified the basis for Simon's sorcery as bitterness—the deepening effect of unforgiveness (v. 2). Here is warning regarding the danger of tolerated or embraced unforgiveness, which may, like poison, permeate and bind the soul, ultimately corrupting everything around it. In Simon's case, his bitterness shaped his passion to control others (v. 19)—which prompted his quest to purchase the ability to impart the gift of the Holy Spirit. Though having believed and been baptized (v. 13), the residue of his past bondage surfaces as he unworthily seeks power to manipulate others for self-exalting purposes. Peter discerns the root of his bondage (v. 23) and summons Simon to repentance and deliverance. Though Simon did not repent, this episode still points to one of the foremost keys to deliverance from entrenched bondage in a believer's soul—the act of _forgiveness_. Forgiving others from our heart flushes out the "poison" with the power of the Cross. In contrast, unforgiveness can, as with Simon, lead down paths we would never have imagined we would travel (see Matt. 6:14, 15; Col. 3:13; Heb. 12:15–17). (Luke 11:24–26/2 Cor. 10:4–6) C.H.

prayed for them ªthat they might receive the Holy Spirit. 16For ªas yet He had fallen upon none of them. ᵇThey had only been baptized in ᶜthe name of the Lord Jesus. 17Then ªthey laid hands on them, and they received the Holy Spirit.

18And when Simon saw that through the laying on of the apostles' hands the Holy Spirit was given, he offered them money, 19saying, "Give me this power also, that anyone on whom I lay hands may receive the Holy Spirit."

20But Peter said to him, "Your money perish with you, because ªyou thought that ᵇthe gift of God could be purchased with money! 21You have neither part nor portion in this matter, for your ªheart is not right in the sight of God. 22Repent therefore of this your wickedness, and pray God ªif perhaps the thought of your heart may be forgiven you. 23For I see that you are ªpoisoned by bitterness and bound by *iniquity."

24Then Simon answered and said, ª"Pray

to the Lord for me, that none of the things which you have spoken may come upon me."

25So when they had testified and preached the word of the Lord, they returned to Jerusalem, preaching the gospel in many villages of the Samaritans.

Christ Is Preached to an Ethiopian

26Now an angel of the Lord spoke to ªPhilip, saying, "Arise and go toward the south along the road which goes down from Jerusalem to Gaza." This is ˡdesert. 27So he arose and went. And behold, ªa man of Ethiopia, a eunuch of great **authority** under Candace the queen of the Ethiopians, who had charge of all her treasury, and ᵇhad

8:15–17 This passage has been subject to unnecessary debate. The sequence of events described in v. 12 leaves little doubt that the Samaritans had become Christians. They had already had a conversion experience with the Holy Spirit, evidenced by their water baptism (vv. 12, 16). Now, through the ministry of the apostles, they are being led into another significant experience with the Holy Spirit, which Luke describes both as "receiving the Holy Spirit," including their allowing Him to "fall upon" them. (See Introduction to Acts: The Holy Spirit at Work for the fluidity of Luke's terms.) This, therefore, may best be seen in the sense of their initial baptism with the Holy Spirit. See also note on 1:5.

8:18–25 Simon evidently **saw** some outward phenomenon that convinced him that the Samaritan converts had received **the Holy Spirit . . . through the laying on of the apostles' hands.**

Although Luke does not identify the external manifestation, many commentators agree that it may likely have been speaking in tongues. **Your money perish. . . . iniquity:** Simon's quest to buy the ability to impart the power of the Spirit was his obvious sin, including a more subtle evil is his desire to use the power of God for his own gain. The word "simony," which is the buying and selling of church offices and influence, originates here. Some ask, Was Simon really saved? "Simon himself also believed" and "was baptized" (v. 13), but Peter's scathing rebuke (v. 21) leaves us uncertain about where Simon really stood with God. Furthermore, the early writings of church history continue to depict Simon as a father of heresies.

8:27 The man of Ethiopia was a high-ranking court official of the queen mother who was a God-fearer, a Gentile who worshiped the Jewish God.

WORD ✦ WEALTH

8:27 authority, *dunastēs;* Strong's #1413: A high official, an important personage, a court official, one invested with power, a ruler, a sovereign, a prince, a royal minister, a potentate. (Cf. "dynasty.") Luke 1:52 suggests that the *dunastēs* of the world systems will be replaced by the Prince of Peace. In Acts 8:27, the *dunastēs* only exists during the reign of Candace, queen of Ethiopia. Jesus' kingdom is a perpetual *dunastēs* without end.

come to Jerusalem to worship, 28was returning. And sitting in his chariot, he was *reading Isaiah the prophet. 29Then the Spirit said to Philip, "Go near and overtake this chariot."

30So Philip ran to him, and heard him reading the *prophet Isaiah, and said, "Do you *understand what you are reading?"

31And he said, "How *can I, unless someone guides me?" And he asked Philip to come up and sit with him. 32The place in the Scripture which he read was this:

a"He was led as a sheep to the slaughter;
And as a lamb before its shearer *is*
silent,
bSo He opened not His mouth.
33 In His humiliation His ajustice* was
taken away,
And who will declare His generation?
For His life is btaken from the earth."

34So the eunuch answered Philip and said, "I ask you, of whom does the prophet say this, of himself or of some other man?" 35Then Philip opened his mouth, aand beginning at this Scripture, preached Jesus to him. 36Now as they went down the road, they came to some water. And the eunuch said, "See, here is water. aWhat hinders me from being baptized?"

37lThen Philip said, a"If you believe with all your *heart, you may."

And he answered and said, b"I believe that Jesus Christ is the Son of God."

38So he commanded the chariot to stand still. And both Philip and the eunuch went

down into the water, and he baptized him. 39Now when they came up out of the water, athe Spirit of the Lord *caught Philip away, so that the eunuch saw him no more; and he went on his way rejoicing. 40But Philip was found at lAzotus. And passing through, he preached in all the cities till he came to aCaesarea.

The Damascus Road: Saul Converted

9 Then aSaul, still breathing threats and murder against the disciples of the Lord, went to the high priest 2and asked aletters from him to the synagogues of Damascus, so that if he found any who were of the Way, whether men or women, he might bring them bound to Jerusalem.

3aAs he journeyed he came near Damascus, and suddenly a light shone around him from heaven. 4Then he fell to the ground, and heard a voice saying to him, "Saul, Saul, awhy are you persecuting Me?"

5And he said, "Who are You, Lord?"

Then the Lord said, "I am Jesus, whom you are persecuting. lIt *is* hard for you to kick against the goads."

6So he, trembling and astonished, said, "Lord, what do You want me to do?"

Then the Lord *said* to him, "Arise and go into the city, and you will be told what you must do."

7And athe men who journeyed with him stood speechless, hearing a voice but *seeing no one. 8Then Saul arose from the ground, and when his eyes were opened he saw no one. But they led him by the hand and brought *him* into Damascus. 9And he was three days without sight, and neither ate nor drank.

Ananias Baptizes Saul

10Now there was a certain disciple at Damascus anamed Ananias; and to him the Lord said in a vision, "Ananias."

And he said, "Here I am, Lord."

11So the Lord *said* to him, "Arise and go to the street called Straight, and inquire at the house of Judas for *one* called Saul aof Tarsus, for behold, he is praying. 12And in

Cross references (center column)

28 *See WW at Mark 13:14.
30 *See WW at Matt. 2:5. • See WW at John 8:32.
31 *See WW at Jude 24.
32 aIs. 53:7, 8 bMatt. 26:62, 63; 27:12, 14; John 19:9
33 aLuke 23:1–25 bLuke 23:33–46 *See WW at Matt. 5:22.
35 aLuke 24:27; Acts 17:2; 18:28; 28:23
36 aActs 10:47; 16:33
37 aMatt. 28:19; [Mark 16:16; Rom. 10:9, 10] bMatt. 16:16; John 6:69; 9:35, 38; 11:27 lNU, M omit v. 37. It is found in Western texts, including the Latin tradition. *See WW at Rev. 2:23.

39 a1 Kin. 18:12; 2 Kin. 2:16; Ezek. 3:12, 14; 2 Cor. 12:2 *See WW at 1 Thess. 4:17.
40 aActs 21:8 lSame as Heb. Ashdod

CHAPTER 9
1 aActs 7:57; 8:1, 3; 26:10, 11; Gal. 1:13; 1 Tim. 1:13
2 aActs 22:5
3 aActs 22:6; 26:12, 13; 1 Cor. 15:8
4 a[Matt. 25:40]
5 lNU, M omit the rest of v. 5 and begin v. 6 with *But arise and go*
7 aDan. 10:7; John 12:29; [Acts 22:9; 26:13] *See WW at John 20:14.
10 aActs 22:12
11 aActs 21:39; 22:3

8:28 Reading in the ancient world was almost always done aloud. During his stay in Jerusalem, this man had probably heard about the resurrection of Christ and the unusual events of Pentecost, and now he was reading from an **Isaiah** scroll, specifically about the sacrificial death of the Messiah (Acts 8:32, 33).

8:38 See note on 2:38.

8:39, 40 Philip was miraculously transported away by the **Spirit of the Lord.** He next appears in Acts 20 years later, still in Caesarea (21:8).

9:1–19 This is the first of three accounts in Acts of Paul's conversion to Christ (see 22:6–21; 26:12–18).

9:1 Paul earnestly believed he was doing the right thing. A num-

ber of OT zealots, like Elijah (see 1 Kin. 18:40), used violence to purge Israel from false religion.

9:4 Saul was not just persecuting people; he was opposing Christ (see Matt. 25:40, 45).

9:5 A goad is a pointed stick for urging on a team of oxen. This may mean that Paul was already having his conscience pricked about the terrible things he was doing.

9:6 Many consider Paul's dramatic conversion to be one of the two great proofs of the validity of the Christian religion, the other being the resurrection of Christ. These two key events are the footings of the Book of Acts.

9:7 See note on 22:9.

a vision he has seen a man named Ananias coming in and putting *his* hand on him, so that he might receive his sight."

13Then Ananias answered, "Lord, I have heard from many about this man, [a]how much [1]harm he has done to Your saints in Jerusalem. 14And here he has authority from the chief priests to bind all [a]who call on Your name."

15But the Lord said to him, "Go, for [a]he is a chosen vessel of Mine to bear My name before [b]Gentiles, [c]kings, and the [d]children[1] of Israel. 16For [a]I will show him how many things he must suffer for My [b]name's sake."

17[a]And Ananias went his way and entered the house; and [b]laying his hands on him he said, "Brother Saul, the Lord

KINGDOM DYNAMICS

9:17 The Apostle Paul Is Filled with the Holy Spirit, HOLY SPIRIT FULLNESS. Saul of Tarsus was filled with the Holy Spirit as a result of Ananias's receiving a vision (v. 10). Saul (later Paul the apostle) was filled with the Holy Spirit as Ananias laid hands on him. The accompanying sign recorded here was the return of Saul's sight (v. 18). Some also note that the apostle Paul valued the fact that he spoke with other tongues (1 Cor. 14:18), so the absence of mentioning as much here might be interpreted as (1) evidence of the commonality of this experience in the early church—not necessarily requiring mention every time; or (2) that this followed later in Paul's experience. (Acts 8:14/Acts 10:44–48) S.G.B.

WORD WEALTH

9:20 preached, *kerussō*; Strong's #2784: To herald, tell abroad, publish, propagate, publicly proclaim, exhort, call out with a clear voice, communicate, preach. The herald is to give a public announcement of an official message and to issue whatever demands the message entails. The Christian herald is to proclaim the message of salvation through Jesus Christ and issue a summons to repent and receive forgiveness of sins.

Cross-references

13 [a]Acts 9:1
[1]*bad things*
14 [a]Acts 7:59; 9:2, 21; 1 Cor. 1:2; 2 Tim. 2:22
15 [a]Acts 13:2; 22:21; Rom. 1:1; 1 Cor. 15:10; Gal. 1:15; Eph. 3:7, 8; 1 Tim. 2:7; 2 Tim. 1:11 [b]Rom. 1:5; 11:13; Gal. 2:7, 8 [c]Acts 25:22, 23; 26:1 [d]Acts 21:40; Rom. 1:16; 9:1–5 [1]*Lit. sons*
16 [a]Acts 20:23; 2 Cor. 11:23–28; 12:7–10; Gal. 6:17; Phil. 1:29, 30 [b]2 Cor. 4:11
17 [a]Acts 22:12, 13 [b]Acts 8:17

[c]Acts 2:4; 4:31; 8:17; 13:52 [1]M omits *Jesus*
*See WW at John 20:21.
19 [a]Acts 26:20
20 [1]NU *Jesus*
21 [a]Acts 8:3; 9:13; Gal. 1:13, 23
22 [a]Acts 18:28
*See WW at 1 Tim. 1:12.
23 [a]Acts 23:12; 2 Cor. 11:26
24 [a]2 Cor. 11:32
25 [a]Josh. 2:15; 1 Sam. 19:12
26 [a]Acts 22:17–20; 26:20; Gal. 1:17, 18
27 [a]Acts 4:36; 13:2 [b]Acts 9:20, 22
28 [a]Gal. 1:18
29 [a]Acts 6:1; 11:20 [b]Acts 9:23; 2 Cor. 11:26 [1]*Greek-speaking Jews*

[1]Jesus, who appeared to you on the road as you came, has *sent me that you may receive your sight and [c]be filled with the Holy Spirit." 18Immediately there fell from his eyes *something* like scales, and he received his sight at once; and he arose and was baptized.

19So when he had received food, he was strengthened. [a]Then Saul spent some days with the disciples at Damascus.

Saul Preaches Christ

20Immediately he **preached** [1]the Christ in the synagogues, that He is the Son of God. 21Then all who heard were amazed, and said, [a]"Is this not he who destroyed those who called on this name in Jerusalem, and has come here for that purpose, so that he might bring them bound to the chief priests?"

22But Saul increased all the more in *strength, [a]and confounded the Jews who dwelt in Damascus, proving that this *Jesus* is the Christ.

Saul Escapes Death

23Now after many days were past, [a]the Jews plotted to kill him. 24[a]But their plot became known to Saul. And they watched the gates day and night, to kill him. 25Then the disciples took him by night and [a]let *him* down through the wall in a large basket.

Saul at Jerusalem

26And [a]when Saul had come to Jerusalem, he tried to join the disciples; but they were all afraid of him, and did not believe that he was a disciple. 27[a]But Barnabas took him and brought *him* to the apostles. And he declared to them how he had seen the Lord on the road, and that He had spoken to him, [b]and how he had preached boldly at Damascus in the name of Jesus. 28So [a]he was with them at Jerusalem, coming in and going out. 29And he spoke boldly in the name of the Lord Jesus and disputed against the [a]Hellenists,[1] [b]but they attempted to kill him. 30When the brethren found out, they brought him down to Caesarea and sent him out to Tarsus.

9:13 Ananias was understandably reluctant about God's command, but the message was clear that he must go (v. 15).

9:16 How many things he must suffer: The call to ministry is bittersweet. See how Paul later describes the ministry in 2 Cor. 4:7–12.

9:17 Be filled with the Holy Spirit: It is generally agreed that Paul was converted three days earlier when he encountered the Lord (vv. 1–9). This experience then, which also included his apostolic commissioning, was likely Paul's initial "baptism with the Holy Spirit." See note on 1:5.

9:22 The church's greatest opponent became her greatest advocate.

9:23 After many days: Paul was in Arabia for three years after his conversion (see Gal. 1:18), some of that time having been spent in Damascus.

9:27 Barnabas means "Son of Consolation," which aptly describes his ministry here, bringing Paul and his former victims together.

9:29 Paul evidently spoke in the same synagogue where Stephen had spoken (see 6:9). The tables are now turned as Paul becomes the target of vicious persecution. The prediction of v. 16 has already begun.

The Church Prospers

31[a]Then the [1]churches throughout all Judea, Galilee, and Samaria had peace and were [b]edified.[2] And walking in the [c]fear of the Lord and in the [d]comfort* of the Holy Spirit, they were [e]multiplied.

Aeneas Healed

32Now it came to pass, as Peter went [a]through all *parts of the country,* that he also came down to the saints who dwelt in Lydda. **33**There he found a certain man named Aeneas, who had been bedridden eight years and was paralyzed. **34**And Peter said to him, "Aeneas, [a]Jesus the Christ heals you. Arise and make your bed." Then he arose immediately. **35**So all who dwelt at Lydda and [a]Sharon saw him and [b]turned to the Lord.

Dorcas Restored to Life

36At Joppa there was a certain disciple named [1]Tabitha, which is translated [2]Dorcas. This woman was full [a]of good works and charitable deeds which she did. **37**But it happened in those days that she became sick and died. When they had washed her,

31 [a]Acts 5:11; 8:1; 16:5 [b][Eph. 4:16, 29] [c]Ps. 34:9 [d]John 14:16 [e]Acts 16:5 [1]NU *church ... was* [2]*built up* *See WW at 2 Cor. 1:5.
32 [a]Acts 8:14
34 [a][Acts 3:6, 16; 4:10]
35 [a]1 Chr. 5:16; 27:29; Is. 33:9; 35:2; 65:10 [b]Acts 11:21; 15:19
36 [a]1 Tim. 2:10; Titus 3:8 [1]Lit., in Aram., *Gazelle* [2]Lit., in Gr., *Gazelle*

37 [a]Acts 1:13; 9:39

9:36 Practical Ministry (Dorcas), BIBLICAL WOMEN. Dorcas was a devout and compassionate woman whose acts of generosity improved the quality of life for the disenfranchised in the community. Her concern extended beyond prayer to various sorts of practical service. She is noted for her aid to the poor, in particular to widows, for whom she served and did noble deeds (Prov. 31:20). The great display of sorrow at her sudden death showed the level of esteem held for her and conveyed her value in the community (Heb. 6:10). The urgent plea to Peter, who raised her from the dead, speaks of the integral role God had given her in meeting the needs of those who relied on her acts of charity (Prov. 19:17; Matt. 25:40). Through her ministry of service, the faith community experienced the manifested love of God. (John 4:28, 29/Acts 21:9) B.A.

they laid *her* in [a]an upper room. **38**And since Lydda was near Joppa, and the disciples had heard that Peter was there, they sent two men to him, imploring *him* not to delay in coming to them. **39**Then Peter arose and went with them. When he had

9:32 Lydda, known as Lod today, was a small village west of Jerusalem on the way to Joppa (see v. 38).

9:34, 35 Aeneas was the recipient of a great blessing, but v. 35 indicates that the healing was really designed to bring many to Christ. The miracle was not just a marvel; it was a sign.

9:36 Joppa was just south of modern Tel Aviv.

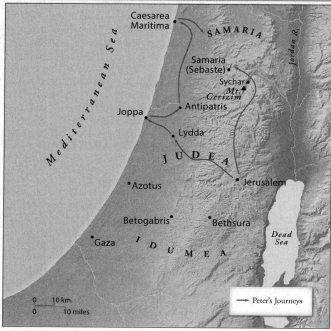

◄ Two journeys are recorded in Acts 8:14–25 and 9:32—10:48.

come, they brought *him* to the upper room. And all the widows stood by him weeping, showing the tunics and garments which Dorcas had made while she was with them. [40]But Peter [a]put them all out, and [b]knelt down and prayed. And turning to the body he [c]said, "Tabitha, arise." And she opened her eyes, and when she saw Peter she sat up. [41]Then he gave her *his* hand and lifted her up; and when he had called the saints and widows, he presented her alive. [42]And it became known throughout all Joppa, [a]and many believed on the Lord. [43]So it was that he stayed many days in Joppa with [a]Simon, a tanner.

Cornelius Sends a Delegation

10 There was a certain man in [a]Caesarea called Cornelius, a centurion of what was called the Italian [1]Regiment, [2][a]a devout *man* and one who [b]feared* God with all his household, who gave [1]alms generously to the people, and prayed to God always. [3]About [1]the ninth hour of the day [a]he saw clearly in a vision an angel of God coming in and saying to him, "Cornelius!"

[4]And when he observed him, he was afraid, and said, "What is it, lord?"

So he said to him, "Your prayers and your alms have come up for a memorial before God. [5]Now [a]send men to Joppa, and send for Simon whose surname is Peter. [6]He is lodging with [a]Simon, a tanner, whose house is by the sea. [b]He[1] will tell you what you must do." [7]And when the angel who spoke to him

had departed, Cornelius called two of his household servants and a devout soldier from among those who waited on him continually. [8]So when he had explained all *these* things to them, he sent them to Joppa.

Peter's Vision

[9]The next day, as they went on their journey and drew near the city, [a]Peter went up on the housetop to *pray, about [1]the sixth hour. [10]Then he became very hungry and wanted to eat; but while they made ready, he fell into a trance [11]and [a]saw heaven opened and an object like a great sheet bound at the four corners, descending to him and let down to the earth. [12]In it were all kinds of four-footed animals of the earth, wild beasts, creeping things, and birds of the air. [13]And a voice came to him, "Rise, Peter; kill and eat." [14]But Peter said, "Not so, Lord! [a]For I have never eaten anything common or unclean." [15]And a voice *spoke* to him again the second time, [a]"What God has [1]cleansed you must not call common." [16]This was done three times. And the object was taken up into heaven again.

Summoned to Caesarea

[17]Now while Peter [1]wondered within himself what this vision which he had seen meant, behold, the men who had been sent from Cornelius had made inquiry for Simon's house, and stood before the gate. [18]And they called and asked whether Simon, whose surname was Peter, was lodging there. [19]While Peter thought about the vision, [a]the *Spirit said to him, "Behold, three men are seeking you. [20][a]Arise therefore, go down and go with them, *doubting nothing; for I have sent them." [21]Then Peter went down to the men [1]who had been sent to him from Cornelius, and said, "Yes, I am he whom you seek. For what reason have you come?"

[22]And they said, "Cornelius *the* centurion, a just man, one who fears God and [a]has a good reputation among all the nation of the Jews, was divinely instructed by a holy angel to summon you to his house, and to hear words from you." [23]Then he invited them in and lodged *them.*

Center column references

40 [a]Matt. 9:25
[b]Luke 22:41;
Acts 7:60
[c]Mark 5:41, 42;
John 11:43
42 [a]John 11:45
43 [a]Acts 10:6

CHAPTER 10
1 [a]Acts 8:40;
23:23 [1]Cohort
2 [a]Acts 8:2;
9:22; 22:12
[b][Acts 10:22,
35; 13:16, 26]
[1]charitable gifts
*See WW at
Matt. 10:26.
3 [a]Acts 10:30;
11:13 [3] P.M.
5 [a]Acts 11:13,
14
6 [a]Acts 9:43
[b]Acts 11:14
[1]NU, M omit
the rest of v. 6.

9 [a]Acts 10:9–32;
11:5–14 [1]Noon
*See WW at
Matt. 6:6.
11 [a]Ezek. 1:1;
Matt. 3:16;
Acts 7:56; Rev.
4:1; 19:11
14 [a]Lev. 11:4;
20:25; Deut.
14:3, 7; Ezek.
4:14
15 [a][Matt. 15:11;
Mark 7:19];
Acts 10:28;
[Rom. 14:14];
1 Cor. 10:25;
[1 Tim. 4:4;
Titus 1:15]
[1]Declared
clean
17 [1]was perplexed
19 [a]Acts 11:12
*See WW at
Rom. 7:6.
20 [a]Acts 15:7–9
*See WW at Acts
11:12.
21 [1]NU, M omit
who had been
sent to him
from Cornelius
22 [a]Acts 22:12

10:1 A centurion was a noncommissioned Roman military officer responsible for a hundred men.

10:2 Although he was not a Jewish proselyte, Cornelius believed in Jewish monotheism and ethical teachings. In spite of the fact that he was **devout,** he still needed to hear the way of salvation.

10:9, 10 The sixth hour, noon. The flat roof was the customary place for relaxation and privacy. The Greek word for **trance,** of which the English word "ecstasy" is a transliteration of the Greek word *ekstasis,* a displacing of the individual's ordinary state of mind with an elevated, God-given state for the purpose of

instructing him. This is in line with the prophetic promise of dreams and visions (2:17) given by the Holy Spirit to advance God's redemptive purposes.

10:11–17 Three times Peter saw a vision of ritually unclean animals, and each time a heavenly voice insisted that he eat them in violation of his Jewish convictions. This triple vision was intended to show Peter that God is not a respecter of persons (v. 34) and that he should readily accompany the strangers downstairs to the residence of their Gentile master. Peter probably would not have visited Cornelius's home if God had not spoken to him so directly (see v. 28; 11:2, 3; Gal. 2:11, 12).

On the next day Peter went away with them, [a]and some brethren from Joppa accompanied him.

Peter Meets Cornelius

24And the following day they entered Caesarea. Now Cornelius was waiting for them, and had called together his relatives and close *friends. 25As Peter was coming in, Cornelius met him and fell down at his feet and worshiped *him*. 26But Peter lifted him up, saying, [a]"Stand up; I myself am also a man." 27And as he talked with him, he went in and found many who had come together. 28Then he said to them, "You know how [a]unlawful it is for a Jewish man to keep company with or go to one of another nation. But [b]God has shown me that I should not call any man common or unclean. 29Therefore I came without objection as soon as I was sent for. I ask, then, for what reason have you sent for me?"

30So Cornelius said, [l]"Four days ago I was fasting until this hour; and at the ninth hour I prayed in my house, and behold, [a]a man stood before me [b]in bright clothing, 31and said, 'Cornelius, [a]your prayer has been heard, and [b]your [l]alms are remembered in the sight of God. 32Send therefore to Joppa and call Simon here, whose surname is Peter. He is lodging in the house of Simon, a tanner, by the sea. [l]When he comes, he will speak to you.' 33So I sent to you immediately, and you have done well to come. Now therefore, we are all present before God, to hear all the things commanded you by God."

Preaching to Cornelius' Household

34Then Peter opened *his* mouth and said: [a]"In truth I *perceive that God shows no **partiality**. 35But [a]in every nation whoever fears Him and *works righteousness is [b]accepted by Him. 36The word which *God* sent to the [l]children of Israel, [a]preaching *peace through Jesus Christ—[b]He is Lord of all— 37that *word you know, which was proclaimed throughout all Judea, and [a]began from Galilee after the baptism which John preached: 38how [a]God anointed Jesus of Nazareth with the Holy Spirit and with *power, who [b]went about doing good and healing all who were oppressed by the devil, [c]for God was with Him. 39And we are [a]witnesses of all things which He did both in the land of the Jews and in Jerusalem, whom [l]they [b]killed by hanging on a tree. 40Him [a]God raised up on the third day, and showed Him openly, 41[a]not to all the people, but to witnesses chosen before by God, *even* to us [b]who ate and drank with Him after He arose from the dead. 42And [a]He commanded us to preach to the people, and to testify [b]that it is He who was ordained by God *to be* Judge [c]of the living and the dead. 43 [a]To Him all the prophets *witness that, through His name, [b]whoever believes in Him will receive [c]remission[l]* of sins."

The Holy Spirit Falls on the Gentiles

44While Peter was still speaking these words, [a]the Holy Spirit fell upon all those

23 [a]Acts 10:45; 11:12
24 *See WW at John 11:11.
26 [a]Acts 14:14, 15; Rev. 19:10; 22:8
28 [a]John 4:9; 18:28; Acts 11:3; Gal. 2:12 [b][Acts 10:14, 35; 15:8, 9]
30 [a]Acts 1:10 [b]Matt. 28:3; Mark 16:5 [l]NU Four days ago to this hour, at the ninth hour
31 [a]Dan. 10:12 [b]Heb. 6:10 [l]charitable gifts
32 [l]NU omits the rest of v. 32.
34 [a]Deut. 10:17; 2 Chr. 19:7; Rom. 2:11; Gal. 2:6; Eph. 6:9 *See WW at John 1:5.
35 [a]Acts 15:9; [1 Cor. 12; 13; Eph. 2:13] [b]Ps. 15:1, 2 *See WW at John 3:21.
36 [a]Is. 57:19; Eph. 2:14; [Col. 1:20] [b]Matt. 28:18; Acts 2:36; Rom. 10:12; 1 Cor. 15:27 [l]Lit. sons *See WW at Luke 1:79.
37 [a]Luke 4:14 *See WW at Matt. 4:4.
38 [a]Is. 61:1–3; Luke 4:18 [b]Matt. 4:23 [c]John 3:2; 8:29 *See WW at Acts 4:33.
39 [a]Acts 1:8 [b]Acts 2:23 [l]NU, M they also
40 [a]Hos. 6:2; Matt. 12:39, 40; 16:4; 20:19; John 2:19–21; Acts 2:24
41 [a][John 14:17, 19, 22; 15:27] [b]Luke 24:30, 41–43
42 [a]Matt. 28:19 [b]John 5:22, 27; Acts 17:31 [c]Rom. 14:9; 2 Tim. 4:1; 1 Pet. 4:5
43 [a]Is. 42:1; 53:11; 61:1]; Jer. 31:34; Dan. 9:24; Hos. 6:1–3; Mic. 7:18; Zech. 13:1; Mal. 4:2 [b][John 3:16, 18;

Acts 26:18]; Rom. 10:11; Gal. 3:22 [c]Acts 13:38, 39 [l]forgiveness *See WW at Acts 26:22. • See WW at Heb. 9:22.   44 [a]Acts 4:31

KINGDOM 🕊 DYNAMICS

10:44–48 A Miracle with the Gentiles Too!, HOLY SPIRIT FULLNESS. The fact that the Gentile household of Cornelius was included in the outpouring of the Spirit is a fulfillment of the prophecy of Joel 2:28 ("I will pour out My Spirit on all flesh"). The presence of the sign of tongues was particularly significant to the Jews who were accompanying Peter in that they received the Holy Spirit "just as we have" (Acts 10:47). This was later related to the leadership in Jerusalem as evidence that God had truly accepted the Gentiles in the plan of salvation (11:16, 17). The baptism with the Holy Spirit is for all believers (2:38, 39). That these began speaking in tongues as Peter was preaching reveals that the pattern of receiving Holy Spirit baptism is not dependent upon first being baptized in water; however, it does not make water baptism optional for a believer. (Acts 9:17/Acts 19:6) S.G.B.

WORD 🗡 WEALTH

10:34 partiality, *prosōpolēptēs;* Strong's #4381: A receiver of a face, one who takes sides, showing favoritism, exhibiting bias, showing discrimination, showing partiality, treating one person better than another. While society makes distinctions among people, God's love and grace are available for all, and can be received by anyone.

10:34–43 See note on 3:12–26.

10:34 The fact that **God shows no partiality** means that He wants everyone, regardless of their nationality or ethnic orientation, to hear the gospel and believe. In Christ there are no barriers (Gal. 3:26–29).

10:35 Peter is not suggesting that salvation is possible apart from the redemptive work of Christ; rather, he emphasizes that through Christ people of all nations can be saved even if they are not Jews.

10:44–48 Just as the Jewish believers received the Spirit and praised God in tongues at Pentecost, these Gentile believers now received the identical gift (v. 45; 11:15). The Jewish Christians who were present knew that the Gentiles had received the **gift of the Holy Spirit** (v. 45), **for they heard them speak with tongues** (v. 46). That tongues are at least one means of giving evidence to the initial baptism in the Holy Spirit is unmistakably clear here. See note on 2:4.

10:44, 45 See section 2 of Truth in Action at the end of Acts.

who heard the word. [45][a]And [l]those of the circumcision who believed were astonished, as many as came with Peter, [b]because the gift of the Holy Spirit had been poured out on the Gentiles also. [46]For they heard them speak with tongues and *magnify God.

(1) Then Peter answered, [47]"Can anyone forbid water, that these should not be baptized who have received the Holy Spirit [a]just as we *have?*" [48][a]And he commanded them to be baptized [b]in the name of the Lord. Then they asked him to stay a few days.

Peter Defends God's Grace

11 Now the apostles and brethren who were in Judea heard that the Gentiles had also received the word of God. [2]And when Peter came up to Jerusalem, [a]those of the circumcision contended with him, [3]saying, [a]"You went in to uncircumcised men [b]and ate with them!"

[4]But Peter explained *it* to them [a]in order from the beginning, saying: [5][a]"I was in the city of Joppa praying; and in a trance I saw a vision, an object descending like a great sheet, let down from heaven by four corners; and it came to me. [6]When I observed it intently and considered, I saw four-footed animals of the earth, wild beasts, creeping things, and birds of the air. [7]And I heard a voice saying to me, 'Rise, Peter; kill and eat.' [8]But I said, 'Not so, Lord! For nothing common or unclean has at any time entered my mouth.' [9]But the voice answered me again from heaven, 'What God has cleansed you must not call common.' [10]Now this was done three times, and all were drawn up again into heaven. [11]At that very moment, three men stood before the house where I was, having been sent to me from Caesarea. [12]Then [a]the Spirit told me to go with them, **doubting** nothing. Moreover [b]these six brethren accompanied me, and we entered the man's house. [13][a]And he told us how he had seen an angel standing in his house, who said to him, 'Send men to Joppa, and call for Simon whose surname is Peter, [14]who will tell you words by which you and all your household will be saved.' [15]And as I began to speak, the *Holy Spirit fell upon them, [a]as upon us at the beginning. [16]Then I remembered the *word of the Lord, how He said, [a]'John indeed baptized with water, but [b]you shall be baptized with the Holy Spirit.' [17][a]If therefore God gave them the

same gift as *He gave* us when we believed on the Lord Jesus Christ, [b]who was I that I could withstand God?"

[18]When they heard these things they became silent; and they glorified God, saying, [a]"Then God has also *granted to the Gentiles repentance to *life."

Barnabas and Saul at Antioch

[19][a]Now those who were scattered after the persecution that arose over Stephen traveled as far as Phoenicia, Cyprus, and Antioch, preaching the word to no one but the Jews only. [20]But some of them were men from Cyprus and Cyrene, who, when they had come to Antioch, spoke to [a]the Hellenists, preaching the Lord Jesus. [21]And [a]the hand of the Lord was with them, and a great number believed and [b]turned to the Lord.

[22]Then news of these things came to the ears of the church in Jerusalem, and they sent out [a]Barnabas to go as far as Antioch. [23]When he came and had seen the grace of God, he was glad, and [d]encouraged them all that with *purpose of heart they should continue with the Lord. [24]For he was a *good man, [a]full of the Holy Spirit and of *faith. [b]And a great many people were added to the Lord.

[25]Then Barnabas departed for [a]Tarsus to seek Saul. [26]And when he had found him, he brought him to Antioch. So it was that for a whole year they assembled with the church and taught a great many people. And the disciples were first called Christians in Antioch.

Relief to Judea

[27]And in these days [a]prophets came from Jerusalem to Antioch. [28]Then one of them, named [a]Agabus, stood up and showed by the Spirit that there was going to be a great famine throughout all the world, which also

> **WORD WEALTH**
>
> **11:12 doubting,** *diakrinō;* Strong's #1252: Has two definitions: (1) to judge thoroughly; to decide between two or more choices; to make a distinction; to separate two components, elements, or factors; to render a decision; to evaluate carefully; and (2) the word also connotes a conflict with oneself, in the sense of hesitating, having misgivings, doubting, being divided in decision making, or wavering between hope and fear. This is its use here.

10:47, 48 See section 1 of Truth in Action at the end of Acts.

11:4–14 See note on 10:11–17.

11:18 This is a pivotal verse. What happened to Cornelius under the ministry of Peter, and the very positive response of the

Jerusalem church, set the stage for Paul's extensive ministry to the Gentiles in the remaining chapters.

11:19 Periodically, the Jews had been forcibly relocated during the previous centuries, and they had established worship and teaching centers in order to maintain their religious and cultural

KINGDOM DYNAMICS

11:27–30 The Office of the Prophet, PROPH-ECY. Agabus is an example of the "office" of the "prophet" in the NT. This role differs from the operation of the gift of prophecy in the life of the believer, for it entails a Christ-appointed ministry *of* a person rather than the Holy Spirit-distributed gift *through* a person. In the NT, this office was not sensationalized as it tends to be today. Such an attitude is unworthy, both in the prophet and in those to whom he ministers, and is certain to result in an unfruitful end. (Apparently, Paul was addressing such assumption of the prophetic office when he issued the challenge of 1 Corinthians 14:37, calling for submission to spiritual authority rather than self-serving independence.) The office of prophet cannot be taken lightly. There is nothing in the NT that reduces the stringent requirements for serving this role, and Deuteronomy 18:20–22 ought to be regarded seriously. Prophecy is nothing to be "experimented" with, for souls are in the balance in the exercise of every ministry.

Further wisdom may be gained by noting that on biblical terms there is more than one type of ministry by a prophet. While a few exercised remarkable predictive gifts (Daniel, Zechariah, John), other traits of the prophetic office are seen: (1) preaching—especially at a national or international level (John the Baptist); (2) teaching—especially when unusual insight is present and broad impact made in serving God's people (Ezra); (3) miracles—as remarkable signs to accompany a prophet's preaching (Elijah); (4) renewal—as with Samuel (1 Sam. 3:21; 4:1), or that called for by the psalmist and by Amos (Ps. 74:9; Amos 8:11, 12). The incident of Agabus resulted in effective action by the church's rising to meet a challenging situation. This is a valid test of the prophetic office. It is for edification and not for entertainment—to enlarge and refresh the body, whether locally or beyond. (Acts 21:11/ Deut. 28:1) J.W.H.

28 ^bActs 18:2
29 ^aRom. 15:26;
1 Cor. 16:1;
2 Cor. 9:1
30 ^aActs 12:25

CHAPTER 12
2 ^aMatt. 4:21;
20:23
3 ^aEx. 12:15;
23:15; Acts
20:6
4 ^aJohn 21:18
¹Gr. *tetrads*,
squads of four
5 ¹NU *constantly*
or earnestly

happened in the days of ^bClaudius Caesar. 29Then the disciples, each according to his ability, determined to send ^arelief to the brethren dwelling in Judea. 30^aThis they also did, and sent it to the elders by the hands of Barnabas and Saul.

Herod's Violence to the Church

12 Now about that time Herod the king stretched out *his* hand to harass some from the church. 2Then he killed James ^athe brother of John with the sword. 3And because he saw that it pleased the Jews, he proceeded further to seize Peter also. Now it was *during* ^athe Days of Unleavened Bread. 4So ^awhen he had arrested him, he put *him* in prison, and delivered *him* to four ¹squads of soldiers to keep him, intending to bring him before the people after Passover.

Peter Freed from Prison

⑶ 5Peter was therefore kept in prison, but ¹constant prayer was offered to God for him

6 ¹*guarding*
7 ^aActs 5:19
9 ^aPs. 126:1
^bActs 10:3, 17;
11:5
*See WW at
John 13:36. ·
See WW at
Rom. 3:4.
10 ^aActs 5:19;
16:26
11 ^a[Ps. 34:7];
Dan. 3:28;
6:22; [Heb.
1:14] ^bJob
5:19; [Ps.
33:18, 19;
34:22; 41:2];
2 Cor. 1:10;
[2 Pet. 2:9]
12 ^aActs 4:23

by the church. 6And when Herod was about to bring him out, that night Peter was sleeping, bound with two chains between two soldiers; and the guards before the door were ¹keeping the prison. 7Now behold, ^aan angel of the Lord stood by *him,* and a light shone in the prison; and he struck Peter on the side and raised him up, saying, "Arise quickly!" And his chains fell off *his* hands. 8Then the angel said to him, "Gird yourself and tie on your sandals"; and so he did. And he said to him, "Put on your garment and follow me." 9So he went out and *followed him, ^adid not know that what was done by the angel was *real, but thought ^bhe was seeing a vision. 10When they were past the first and the second guard posts, they came to the iron gate that leads to the city, ^awhich opened to them of its own accord; and they went out and went down one street, and immediately the angel departed from him. 11And when Peter had come to himself, he said, "Now I know for certain that ^athe Lord has sent His angel, and ^bhas delivered me from the hand of Herod and *from* all the expectation of the Jewish people." 12So, when he had considered *this,* ^ahe came to the house of Mary, the mother of

identity. Missionary work out of the Jerusalem church was at first limited exclusively to these synagogues of the Dispersion.

11:26 Christians is a transliteration of the Greek *christianos,* which was a simple, and most likely a derisive name given to the early followers of Christ (Gr. *christos*), not unlike a believer's today being called a "Jesus-person" in an uncomplimentary way.

11:28 Apparently, predictive prophecy about specific future events was the exclusive ministry of "the prophet," while in 1 Cor. 14:1 Paul encouraged everyone to prophesy for the general edification or encouragement of the church (1 Cor. 14:3). The Scriptures, then, seem to distinguish between the gift of prophecy and the office of the prophet. **Claudius Caesar** was the Roman emperor in A.D. 41–54. The Jewish historian Josephus records a famine that occurred in Judea in A.D. 46.

12:1 Herod is Herod Agrippa I (A.D. 37–44), grandson of Herod the Great. Little is recorded about this man in Scripture, but it is known that he had helped Claudius become emperor of Rome after the notorious Emperor Caligula was murdered. Herod Agrippa I suffered an untimely and humiliating death (vv. 20–24). By including this account here Luke may be showing a connection between the death of Herod and his persecution of Christians.

12:2 James was the first of the twelve apostles to be martyred.

12:3 Days of Unleavened Bread was a part of the Passover festival in the spring (see v. 4 and Lev. 23:4–8).

12:4 Four squads was sixteen soldiers.

12:5 See section 3 of Truth in Action at the end of Acts.

[b]John whose surname was Mark, where many were gathered together [c]praying. [13]And as Peter knocked at the door of the gate, a girl named Rhoda came to answer. [14]When she *recognized Peter's voice, because of *her* gladness she did not open the gate, but ran in and announced that Peter stood before the gate. [15]But they said to her, "You are beside yourself!" Yet she kept insisting that it was so. So they said, [a]"It is his angel."

[16]Now Peter continued knocking; and when they opened *the door* and saw him, they were astonished. [17]But [a]motioning to them with his hand to keep silent, he declared to them how the Lord had brought him out of the prison. And he said, "Go, tell these things to James and to the brethren." And he departed and went to another place.

[18]Then, as soon as it was day, there was no small [1]stir among the soldiers about what had become of Peter. [19]But when Herod had searched for him and not found him, he examined the guards and commanded that *they* should be put to death.

And he went down from Judea to Caesarea, and stayed *there.*

Herod's Violent Death

[20]Now Herod had been very angry with the people of [a]Tyre and Sidon; but they came to him *with one accord, and having made Blastus [1]the king's personal aide their friend, they asked for peace, because [b]their country was [2]supplied with food by the king's *country.*

[21]So on a set day Herod, arrayed in royal apparel, sat on his *throne and gave an oration to them. [22]And the people kept shouting, "The voice of a god and not of a man!" [23]Then immediately an angel of the Lord [a]struck him, because [b]he did not give glory to God. And he was eaten by worms and [i]died.

[24]But [a]the word of God grew and multiplied.

Barnabas and Saul Appointed

[25]And [a]Barnabas and Saul returned [1]from Jerusalem when they had [b]fulfilled

Cross references (center column)

12 [b]Acts 13:5, 13; 15:37; 2 Tim. 4:11; Philem. 24; 1 Pet. 5:13
[c]Acts 12:5
14 *See WW at Luke 5:22.
15 [a]Gen. 48:16; [Matt. 18:10]
17 [a]Acts 13:16; 19:33; 21:40
18 [1]disturbance
20 [a]Matt. 11:21
[b]1 Kin. 5:11; Ezra 3:7; Ezek. 27:17 [1]who was in charge of the king's bedchamber
[2]Lit. nourished
*See WW at Acts 2:1.
21 *See WW at Matt. 27:19.
23 [a]1 Sam. 25:38; 2 Sam. 24:16, 17; 2 Kin. 19:35; Acts 5:19
[b]Ps. 115:1
[i]breathed his last
24 [a]Is. 55:11; Acts 6:7; 19:20
25 [a]Acts 11:30
[b]Acts 11:30
[1]NU, M to

12:17 James was the Lord's half brother (see Mark 6:3), who became the leader of the Jerusalem church (Acts 15:13; 21:18) and who wrote the Epistle of James. Paul refers to him as one of the "pillars" of the church (Gal. 2:9) and as an apostle (Gal. 1:19).

12:20–23 See note on v. 1. The first-century Jewish historian Josephus corroborates Luke's account of Herod's unusual death.

Neither Luke nor Josephus gives enough details to determine the exact medical cause the divine judgment incurred. It may have been peritonitis or an intestinal obstruction. **He was eaten by worms and died** references the humiliation surrounding his death, not the means of his demise.

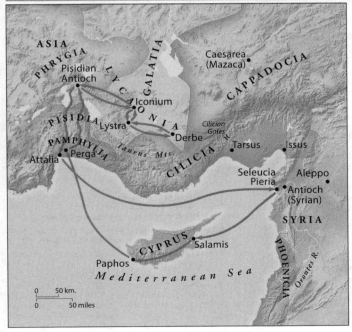

PAUL GOES TO GALATIA (THE FIRST MISSIONARY JOURNEY, ACTS 13:1—14:28)

◄ Sent out from the church at Antioch (Acts 13:1–3), Paul and Barnabas went to the cities of Galatia in Asia Minor. The Jewish synagogues in these cities provided Paul a platform for preaching the gospel. At times, however, he even encountered opposition from the synagogues.

WORD ✝ WEALTH

13:2 ministered, *leitourgeō;* Strong's #3008: Performing religious or charitable acts, fulfilling an office, discharging a function, officiating as a priest, serving God with prayers and fastings. (Cf. "liturgy" and "liturgical.") The word describes the Aaronic priesthood ministering Levitical services (Heb. 10:11). In Romans 15:27, it is used of meeting financial needs of the Christians, performing a service to the Lord by doing so. Here the Christians at Antioch were fulfilling an office and discharging a normal function by ministering to the Lord in fasting and prayer.

their ministry, and they also ᶜtook with them ᵈJohn whose surname was Mark.

③ **13** Now ᵃin the church that was at Antioch there were certain prophets and teachers: ᵇBarnabas, Simeon who was called Niger, ᶜLucius of Cyrene, Manaen who had been brought up with Herod the tetrarch, and Saul. 2As they **ministered** to the Lord and fasted, the Holy Spirit said, ᵃ"Now separate to Me Barnabas and Saul for the work ᵇto which I have called them." 3Then, ᵃhaving fasted and prayed, and laid hands on them, they sent *them* away.

Preaching in Cyprus

4So, being sent out by the Holy Spirit, they went down to Seleucia, and from there they sailed to ᵃCyprus. 5And when they arrived in Salamis, ᵃthey preached the word of God in the synagogues of the Jews. They also had ᵇJohn as *their* assistant.

6Now when they had gone through ˡthe island to Paphos, they found ᵃa certain sorcerer, a false prophet, a Jew whose name *was* Bar-Jesus, 7who was with the

---

25 ᶜActs 13:5, 13
ᵈActs 12:12;
15:37

CHAPTER 13
1 ᵃActs 14:26
ᵇActs 11:22
ᶜRom. 16:21
2 ᵃNum. 8:14;
Acts 9:15;
22:21; Rom.
1:1; Gal. 1:15;
2:9 ᵇMatt.
9:38; Acts
14:26; Rom.
10:15; Eph. 3:7,
8; 1 Tim. 2:7;
2 Tim. 1:11;
Heb. 5:4
3 ᵃMatt. 9:15;
Mark 2:20;
Luke 5:35;
Acts 6:6
4 ᵃActs 4:36
5 ᵃ[Acts 13:46]
ᵇActs 12:25;
15:37
6 ᵃActs 8:9 ˡNU
the whole
island

8 ᵃEx. 7:11;
2 Tim. 3:8
ˡopposed
*See WW at Eph.
6:13.
9 ᵃActs 2:4; 4:8
10 ᵃMatt. 13:38;
John 8:44;
[1 John 3:8]
11 ᵃEx. 9:3;
1 Sam. 5:6;
Job 19:21;
Ps. 32:4; Heb.
10:31
*See WW at
Luke 11:35.
13 ᵃActs 15:38
14 ᵃActs 16:13
15 ᵃLuke 4:16
ᵇHeb. 13:22
ˡencourage-
ment
16 ᵃActs 10:35
17 ᵃEx. 6:1, 6;
13:14, 16;
Deut. 7:6–8
ᵇActs 7:17 ᶜEx.
14:8 ˡM omits
Israel ²Mighty
power
18 ᵃEx. 16:35;
Num. 14:34;
Acts 7:36

---

proconsul, Sergius Paulus, an intelligent man. This man called for Barnabas and Saul and sought to hear the word of God. 8But ᵃElymas the sorcerer (for so his name is translated) ˡwithstood* them, seeking to turn the proconsul away from the faith. 9Then Saul, who also *is called* Paul, ᵃfilled ② with the Holy Spirit, looked intently at him 10and said, "O full of all deceit and all fraud, ᵃ*you* son of the devil, *you* enemy of all righteousness, will you not cease perverting the straight ways of the Lord? 11And now, indeed, ᵃthe hand of the Lord *is* upon you, and you shall be blind, not seeing the sun for a time."

And immediately a *dark mist fell on him, and he went around seeking someone to lead him by the hand. 12Then the proconsul believed, when he saw what had been done, being astonished at the teaching of the Lord.

At Antioch in Pisidia

13Now when Paul and his party set sail from Paphos, they came to Perga in Pamphylia; and ᵃJohn, departing from them, returned to Jerusalem. 14But when they departed from Perga, they came to Antioch in Pisidia, and ᵃwent into the synagogue on the Sabbath day and sat down. 15And ᵃafter the reading of the Law and the Prophets, the rulers of the synagogue sent to them, saying, "Men *and* brethren, if you have ᵇany word of ˡexhortation for the people, say on."

16Then Paul stood up, and motioning with *his* hand said, "Men of Israel, and ᵃyou who fear God, listen: 17The God of this people ˡIsrael ᵃchose our fathers, and exalted the people ᵇwhen they dwelt as **strangers** in the land of Egypt, and with ²an uplifted arm He ᶜbrought them out of it. 18Now ᵃfor a time of about forty years He **put up with**

13:1–3 See section 3 of Truth in Action at the end of Acts.

13:1 Simeon is not mentioned anywhere else in the Bible. Some commentators speculate he may have been the same person as Simon of Cyrene, the man who bore Jesus' cross (Luke 23:26). **Manaen who had been brought up with Herod:** perhaps they were childhood friends. This suggests that he was probably a man of distinction. **Prophets and teachers:** See note on Eph. 4:11.

13:2, 3 This is the commissioning of Paul's great apostolic ministry. **Ministered** translates a verb used of the official service of priests. Here it speaks of their ministry of public worship. They **fasted:** Fasting is a spiritual exercise, a voluntary restraint from food for the purpose of seeking God. Jesus' own teaching encouraged this practice (Matt. 9:15; Luke 5:35). **The Holy Spirit** probably spoke in a prophecy uttered by one of the "prophets" (Acts 13:1). **Laid hands on them** is an act of spiritual impartation and commissioning.

13:4 This is the beginning of Paul's first missionary journey, which ends in 14:26–28. See map of Paul's first journey.

13:6 Bar-Jesus means "Son of Jesus," but suggests no relationship to our Lord. Jesus, or Joshua, was a common name at the time.

13:7 The Roman Empire was divided into (1) imperial provinces, which were administrated by appointed representatives of the emperor called procurators (as Pilate in Judea), and (2) senatorial

provinces, which were presided over by proconsuls appointed by the Roman senate. **Sergius Paulus** was the **proconsul** of the island of Cyprus.

13:9–11 The fact that Luke attributes Paul's rebuke to the fullness of **the Holy Spirit** indicates he is acting as God's mediatorial agent of divine judgment, not speaking forth personal judgment or vindictiveness. See 5:1–11; Rom. 1:28; 2:5.

13:9 See section 2 of Truth in Action at the end of Acts.

13:9 See note on 4:8.

13:12 Astonished at the teaching of the Lord: This does not refer to the mere presentation of religious truths. The proconsul was astonished at the power of the teaching (see Mark 1:22).

13:14 Antioch was located in present-day Turkey, and is not the same as Antioch in Syria from which Paul was sent in v. 1.

13:15 Jewish synagogues were open forums, and it was quite proper for guests to speak and teach.

13:17–41 A typical Acts sermon (see note on 3:12–26), including (1) a review of Jewish history (vv. 17–22); (2) a sketch of the life of Christ (vv. 23–31) with an emphasis on His Resurrection (vv. 30, 33, 34); (3) OT texts to prove that Jesus is the Messiah (vv. 32–37); and (4) a call to hear the message, repent, and believe (vv. 38–41). **Justified** (v. 39) here has the idea of being set free.

WORD WEALTH

13:17 strangers, *paroikia;* Strong's #3940: Aliens, foreigners, strangers, sojourners, noncitizens dwelling as resident exiles. (Cf. "parochial" and "parish.") Israel sojourned in Egypt on a *paroikia* basis. Their permanent home was the land of Canaan. First Peter 1:17 uses *paroikia* in the spiritual sense. Christians live temporarily as aliens in an unfriendly world. The Lord has prepared for them a final home based on permanency, duration, and endless time.

WORD WEALTH

13:18 put up with, *tropophoreō;* Strong's #5159: This Greek word, which occurs only here in the NT, means "to bear with." But other manuscripts read "cared for" (lit. "carried them as a nurse"). The two Greek words differ in only one letter: *etrophophorēsen* ("nourished") and *etropophorēsen* ("bore with"). "Nourished" is probably a quote from the Septuagint (Greek OT) translation of Deuteronomy 1:31. With that as the reading, Paul in this sermon to Jews at Antioch was emphasizing God's great care for the Israelites in the wilderness. Otherwise, Paul was using the expression "He put up with" as a graphic portrayal of God's patience.

their ways in the wilderness. 19And when He had destroyed ᵃseven nations in the land of Canaan, ᵇHe distributed their land to them by allotment.

20"After that ᵃHe gave *them* judges for about four hundred and fifty years, ᵇuntil Samuel the prophet. 21ᵃAnd afterward they asked for a king; so God gave them ᵇSaul the son of Kish, a man of the tribe of Benjamin, for forty years. 22And ᵃwhen He had *removed him, ᵇHe raised up for them David as king, to whom also He gave testimony and said, ᶜ'I have found David the *son* of Jesse, ᵈa man after My *own* heart, who will do all My *will.' 23ᵃFrom this man's seed, according ᵇto *the promise, God raised up for Israel ᶜa¹ *Savior—Jesus— 24ᵃafter John had first preached, before His coming, the baptism of repentance to all the people of Israel. 25And as John was finishing his course, he said, ᵃ'Who do you think I am? I am not *He. But behold, ᵇthere comes One after me, the sandals of whose feet I am not worthy to loose.'

26"Men *and* brethren, sons of the ¹family of Abraham, and ᵃthose among you who fear God, ᵇto you the ²word of this salvation has been sent. 27For those who dwell in Jerusalem, and their rulers, ᵃbecause they

Marginal references (left column):
19 ᵃDeut. 7:1
ᵇJosh. 14:1, 2; 19:51; Ps. 78:55
20 ᵃJudg. 2:16; 1 Sam. 4:18; 7:15 ᵇ1 Sam. 3:20; Acts 3:24
21 ᵃ1 Sam. 8:5 ᵇ1 Sam. 10:20–24
22 ᵃ1 Sam. 15:23, 26, 28 ᵇ1 Sam. 16:1, 12, 13 ᶜPs. 89:20 ᵈ1 Sam. 13:14
*See WW at Luke 16:4. •
See WW at Matt. 12:50.
23 ᵃIs. 11:1 ᵇPs. 132:11 ᶜ[Matt. 1:21] ¹M salvation, after
*See WW at John 4:42.
24 ᵃMatt. 3:1; [Luke 3:3]
25 ᵃMatt. 3:11; Mark 1:7; Luke 3:16 ᵇJohn 1:20, 27
26 ᵃPs. 66:16 ᵇMatt. 10:6 ¹stock ²message
27 ᵃLuke 23:34

28 ᵃMatt. 27:22, 23; Mark 15:13, 14; Luke 23:21–23; John 19:15; Acts 3:14; [2 Cor. 5:21; Heb. 4:15]; 1 Pet. 2:22
29 ᵃLuke 18:31 ᵇMatt. 27:57–61; Mark 15:42–47; Luke 23:50–56; John 19:38–42
30 ᵃPs. 16:10, 11; Hos. 6:2; Matt. 12:39, 40; 28:6
31 ᵃMatt. 28:16; Acts 1:3, 11; 1 Cor. 15:5–8
32 ᵃ[Gen. 3:15]
33 ᵃPs. 2:7; Heb. 1:5
34 ᵃIs. 55:3 ¹the state of decay ²blessings
35 ᵃPs. 16:10; Acts 2:27
36 ᵃActs 2:29 ¹in his ²underwent decay
37 ¹underwent no decay
38 ᵃJer. 31:34
39 ᵃ[Is. 53:11; John 3:16]
*See WW at Matt. 12:37.
41 ᵃHab. 1:5

WORD WEALTH

13:32 promise, *epaggelia;* Strong's #1860: Both a promise and the thing promised, an announcement with the special sense of promise, pledge, and offer. *Epaggelia* tells what the promise from God is and then gives the assurance that the thing promised will be done. 2 Corinthians 1:20 asserts, "For all the promises [*epaggelia*] of God in Him are Yes, and in Him Amen, to the glory of God through us."

did not know Him, nor even the voices of the Prophets which are read every Sabbath, have fulfilled *them* in condemning *Him.* 28ᵃAnd though they found no cause for death *in Him,* they asked Pilate that He should be put to death. 29ᵃNow when they had fulfilled all that was written concerning Him, ᵇthey took *Him* down from the tree and laid *Him* in a tomb. 30ᵃBut God raised Him from the dead. 31ᵃHe was seen for many days by those who came up with Him from Galilee to Jerusalem, who are His witnesses to the people. 32And we declare to you glad tidings—ᵃthat **promise** which was made to the fathers. 33God has fulfilled this for us their children, in that He has raised up Jesus. As it is also written in the second Psalm:

ᵃ'You are My Son,
   Today I have begotten You.'

34And that He raised Him from the dead, no more to return to ¹corruption, He has spoken thus:

ᵃ'I will give you the sure ²mercies of
   David.'

35Therefore He also says in another *Psalm:*

ᵃ'You will not allow Your Holy One to
   see corruption.'

36"For David, after he had served ¹his own generation by the will of God, ᵃfell asleep, was buried with his fathers, and ²saw corruption; 37but He whom God raised up ¹saw no corruption. 38Therefore let it be known to you, brethren, that ᵃthrough this Man is preached to you the forgiveness of sins; 39and ᵃby Him everyone who believes is *justified from all things from which you could not be justified by the law of Moses. 40Beware therefore, lest what has been spoken in the prophets come upon you:

41 'Behold,ᵃ you despisers,
   Marvel and perish!
   For I work a work in your days,

A work which you will by no means
      believe,
Though one were to declare it to you.' "

Blessing and Conflict at Antioch

42[1]So when the Jews went out of the synagogue, the Gentiles begged that these words might be preached to them the next Sabbath. 43Now when the congregation had broken up, many of the Jews and devout proselytes *followed Paul and Barnabas, who, speaking to them, [a]persuaded them to continue in [b]the grace of God.

44On the next Sabbath almost the whole city came together to hear the word of God. 45But when the Jews saw the multitudes, they were filled with envy; and contradicting and blaspheming, they [a]opposed the things spoken by Paul. 46Then Paul and Barnabas grew bold and said, [a]"It was necessary that the word of God should be spoken to you first; but [b]since you reject it, and judge yourselves unworthy of *everlasting life, behold, [c]we turn to the Gentiles. 47For so the Lord has commanded us:

[a]'I have set you as a light to the Gentiles,
    That you should be for salvation to the
        ends of the earth.' "

48Now when the Gentiles heard this, they were glad and glorified the word of the Lord. [a]And as many as had been appointed to eternal life believed.

49And the word of the Lord was being spread throughout all the region. 50But the Jews stirred up the devout and prominent women and the chief men of the city, [a]raised up persecution against Paul and Barnabas, and expelled them from their region. 51[a]But they shook off the dust from their feet against them, and came to Iconium. 52And the disciples [a]were filled with joy and [b]with the Holy Spirit.

At Iconium

14 Now it happened in Iconium that they went together to the synagogue of the Jews, and so spoke that a great multitude

both of the Jews and of the [a]Greeks believed. 2But the unbelieving Jews stirred up the Gentiles and [1]poisoned their [2]minds against the brethren. 3Therefore they stayed there a long time, speaking boldly in the Lord, [a]who was bearing witness to the word of His grace, granting signs and [b]wonders* to be done by their hands.

4But the multitude of the city was [a]divided: part sided with the Jews, and part with the [b]apostles. 5And when a violent attempt was made by both the Gentiles and Jews, with their rulers, [a]to *abuse and stone them, 6they became aware of it and [a]fled to Lystra and Derbe, cities of Lycaonia, and to the surrounding region. 7And they were preaching the gospel there.

Idolatry at Lystra

8[a]And in Lystra a certain man without strength in his feet was sitting, a cripple from his mother's womb, who had never walked. 9*This* man heard Paul speaking. [1]Paul, observing him intently and seeing that he had faith to be healed, 10said with a loud voice, [a]"Stand up straight on your feet!" And he leaped and walked. 11Now when the people saw what Paul had done, they raised their voices, saying in the Lycaonian *language*, [a]"The gods have come down to us in the likeness of men!" 12And Barnabas they called [1]Zeus, and Paul, [2]Hermes, because he was the chief speaker. 13Then the priest of Zeus, whose temple was in front of their city, brought oxen and garlands to the gates, [a]intending to sacrifice with the multitudes.

14But when the apostles Barnabas and Paul heard this, [a]they tore their clothes and ran in among the multitude, crying out 15and saying, "Men, [a]why are you doing these things? [b]We also are men with the same nature as you, and preach to you that you should turn from [c]these **useless** things [d]to the living God, [e]who made the heaven, the earth, the sea, and all things that are in them, 16[a]who in bygone generations allowed

Cross references (center column):

42 [1]Or And when they went out of the synagogue of the Jews; NU And when they went out, they begged
43 [a]Acts 11:23 [b]Titus 2:11; Heb. 12:15; 1 Pet. 5:12
*See WW at John 13:36.
45 [a]Acts 18:6; 1 Pet. 4:4; Jude 10
46 [a]Matt. 10:6; Acts 3:26; Rom. 1:16 [b]Ex. 32:10; Deut. 32:21; Is. 55:5; Matt. 21:43; Rom. 10:19 [c]Acts 18:6
*See WW at Rev. 14:6.
47 [a]Is. 42:6; 49:6; Luke 2:32
48 [a][Acts 2:47]
50 [a]Acts 7:52; 2 Tim. 3:11
51 [a]Matt. 10:14; Mark 6:11; [Luke 9:5]
52 [a]Matt. 5:12; John 16:22 [b]Acts 2:4; 4:8, 31; 13:9

CHAPTER 14
1 [a]John 7:35; Acts 18:4; Rom. 1:14, 16; 1 Cor. 1:22
2 [1]embittered [2]Lit. souls
3 [a]Mark 16:20; Acts 4:29; 20:32; Heb. 2:4 [b]Acts 5:12
*See WW at Acts 15:12.
4 [a]Luke 12:51 [b]Acts 13:2, 3
5 [a]2 Tim. 3:11
*See WW at Luke 18:32.
6 [a]Matt. 10:23
8 [a]Acts 3:2
9 [1]Lit. Who
10 [a][Is. 35:6]
11 [a]Acts 8:10; 28:6
12 [1]Jupiter [2]Mercury
13 [a]Dan. 2:46
14 [a]Num. 14:6; Matt. 26:65; Mark 14:63
15 [a]Acts 10:26 [b]James 5:17 [c]1 Sam. 12:21; Jer. 8:19; 14:22; Amos 2:4; 1 Cor. 8:4 [d]1 Thess. 1:9 [e]Gen. 1:1;
Ex. 20:11; Ps. 146:6; Acts 4:24; 17:24; Rev. 14:7 **16** [a]Ps. 81:12; Mic. 4:5; 1 Pet. 4:3

13:42 The Gentiles here were converts to the Jewish religion.

13:46, 47 These are important transitional verses in the narrative. The preaching of the gospel is beginning to turn away from the Jewish community. Paul began his ministry in each new city by entering the synagogue, but rejection by the Jews forced him to preach to Gentile audiences.

13:48 The primary significance of the phrase **appointed to eternal life** is not theological but historical, as Luke traces the spread of the gospel from its Jewish origins to the Gentile world. This reference underscores God's initiative in individual salvation. Throughout the Bible there are references to God's hand of providence influencing people and altering the course of human history. Every Christian, in retrospect, can see how God carefully orchestrated particular events that changed his life forever. See Prov. 16:9; Dan. 4:34, 35; Acts 2:22–24; Eph. 1:3–5.

13:51 Shook off the dust is a dramatic symbol of divine abandonment. See Matt. 10:14.

13:52 The tense of the verb **were filled** signifies a continuous filling.

14:3 See section 4 of Truth in Action at the end of Acts.

14:9 In both the Gospels and Acts, faith is often emphasized as the condition of healing (see Matt. 8:10; 9:2, 22, 29; 15:28; Mark 10:52; Luke 17:19; Acts 3:16). See Word Wealth at Mark 11:22.

14:12 The worship of **Zeus** and **Hermes** (the father and the messenger of the gods and known to the Romans as Jupiter and Mercury) in ancient Lystra has been established by archaeological research.

14:14–18 See section 3 of Truth in Action at the end of Acts.

WORD WEALTH

14:15 useless, *mataios;* Strong's #*3152:* Fruitless, empty, futile, frivolous, hollow, unreal, unproductive, lacking substance, trifling, ineffectual, void of results, devoid of force, success, or utility, and worthless. The word here describes Greek and Roman mythological ritual. The unregenerate philosophy of that day made Paul and Barnabas urge the people to turn from these useless (*mataios*) things. Their message was "turn from Zeus, who has never lived, to God who has always been alive. As Creator He is worthy to be served, worshiped, and trusted."

all nations to walk in their own ways. [17][a]Nevertheless He did not leave Himself without witness, in that He did good, [b]gave us rain from heaven and fruitful seasons, filling our hearts with [c]food and gladness." [18]And with these sayings they could scarcely restrain the multitudes from sacrificing to them.

Stoning, Escape to Derbe

[19][a]Then Jews from Antioch and Iconium came there; and having persuaded the multitudes, [b]they stoned Paul *and* dragged *him* out of the city, supposing him to be [c]dead. [20]However, when the disciples gathered around him, he rose up and went into the city. And the next day he departed with Barnabas to Derbe.

Strengthening the Converts

[21]And when they had preached the gospel to that city [a]and made many disciples, they returned to Lystra, Iconium, and Antioch, [22]strengthening the souls of the disciples, [a]exhorting *them* to continue in the faith, and *saying,* [b]"We must through many *tribulations enter the kingdom of God." [23]So when they had [a]appointed elders in every church, and prayed with fasting, they commended them to the Lord in whom they had believed. [24]And after they had passed through Pisidia, they came to Pamphylia. [25]Now when they had preached the word in Perga, they went down to Attalia. [26]From

17 [a]Acts 17:24–27; Rom. 1:19, 20 [b]Lev. 26:4; Deut. 11:14; [Matt. 5:45] [c]Ps. 145:16
19 [a]Acts 13:45, 50; 14:2–5; 1 Thess. 2:14 [b]Acts 14:5; 2 Cor. 11:25; 2 Tim. 3:11 [c][2 Cor. 12:1–4]
21 [a]Matt. 28:19
22 [a]Acts 11:23 [b]Matt. 10:38; Luke 22:28; [Rom. 8:17; 2 Tim. 2:12; 3:12]
*See WW at John 16:33.
23 [a]Matt. 9:15; Mark 2:20; Luke 5:35; 2 Cor. 8:19; Titus 1:5

27 [a]Acts 15:4, 12 [b]1 Cor. 16:9; 2 Cor. 2:12; Col. 4:3; Rev. 3:8

CHAPTER 15
1 [a]Gal. 2:12 [b]John 7:22; Acts 15:5; Gal. 5:2; Phil. 3:2; [Col. 2:8, 11, 16]

KINGDOM DYNAMICS

14:21, 22 Suffering, Tribulation, CONFLICT AND THE KINGDOM. Paul not only taught the joy and peace of the kingdom of God (Rom. 14:17), its power (1 Cor. 4:20), and its present authority to cause the believer to triumph over evil (2 Tim. 4:18; Rom. 16:20). He also taught that "kingdom people" experience trial, suffering, and not always an "instant victory" (2 Thess. 1:5). Triumph and victory may characterize the attitude of each citizen of the kingdom of God, and Holy Spirit-empowered authority is given to be applied to realize results. Yet, God did not promise life without struggle. The "dominion" being recovered through the presence of the King within us and ministered by the Holy Spirit's power through us is never taught by the apostles as preempting all suffering.

This text reminds us that victory only comes through battle, and triumph only follows trial. Only a weak view of the truth of the kingdom of God pretends otherwise. Another weak view surrenders to negative circumstances on the proposition that we are predestined to problems and therefore should merely tolerate them. The Bible teaches that suffering, trial, and all order of human difficulty are unavoidable; but God's Word also teaches that they may all be overcome. The presence of the King and the power of His kingdom in our lives make us neither invulnerable nor immune to life's struggles. But they do bring the promise of victory: provision in need, strength for the day, and healing, comfort, and saving help. (Luke 16:16/Ps. 22:3) J.W.H.

there they sailed to Antioch, where they had been commended to the grace of God for the work which they had completed.

[27]Now when they had come and gathered the church together, [a]they reported all that God had done with them, and that He had [b]opened the door of faith to the Gentiles. [28]So they stayed there a long time with the disciples.

Conflict over Circumcision

15 And [a]certain *men* came down from Judea and taught the brethren, [b]"Unless you are circumcised according to the custom of Moses, you cannot be saved."

14:19, 20 Many scholars believe that Paul was describing this near-death experience in 2 Cor. 12:2–5. It is possible that when Paul **rose up and went into the city,** he was actually raised from the dead. At the very least, he was miraculously healed, because **the next day he departed with Barnabas to Derbe.**

14:22 Enduring sufferings does not earn entrance into the kingdom. The meaning is that persecution accompanies entrance into the kingdom.

15:1–35 This section represents a theological milestone in the history of Christianity. All the principal leaders of the early church agreed to meet in Jerusalem to resolve the emerging conflict between legalistic Jewish Christians and Gentile converts to Christianity (vv. 1, 2). The legalists, called Judaizers, believed that in addition to exercising faith in Jesus, one must observe the ceremonial **custom** (v. 1) of the OT, especially the rite of circumcision. Judaizers, then, expected Gentile believers to be circumcised and observe the Law of Moses, just as converts to Judaism had been circumcised for generations previously (v. 21). After **much dispute** (v. 7), the Jerusalem Council agreed on what has become the doctrinal foundation of the Christian faith: Salvation is by grace through faith alone (v. 11). Paul's letter to the Galatians is an extended explanation of this doctrine. See also Rom. 3:28; 2 Cor. 3:7–18; Eph. 2:8, 9; Col. 2:11–17. The clarification of salvation by grace through faith in Jesus Christ alone also led to a final and formal separation of Christianity from Judaism.

15:1 Paul's report of what had happened among the Gentiles on his first missionary journey (14:26–28) had reached Jerusalem

2Therefore, when Paul and Barnabas had no small dissension and dispute with them, they determined that [a]Paul and Barnabas and certain *others of them should go up to Jerusalem, to the apostles and elders, about this question.

3So, [a]being sent on their way by the church, they passed through Phoenicia and Samaria, [b]describing the conversion of the Gentiles; and they caused great joy to all the brethren. 4And when they had come to Jerusalem, they were received by the church and the apostles and the elders; and they reported all things that God had done with them. 5But some of the *sect of the Pharisees who believed rose up, saying, "It is necessary to circumcise them, and to command *them* to keep the law of Moses."

The Jerusalem Council

6Now the apostles and elders came together to consider this matter. 7And when there had been much dispute, Peter rose up *and* said to them: [a]"Men *and* brethren, you know that a good while ago God chose among us, that by my mouth the Gentiles should hear the word of the *gospel and believe. 8So God, [a]who knows the heart, [1]acknowledged them by [b]giving them the Holy Spirit, just as *He did* to us, 9[a]and made no *distinction between us and them, [b]purifying their hearts by faith. 10Now therefore, why do you test God [a]by putting a yoke on the neck of the disciples which neither our fathers nor we were able to bear? 11But [a]we believe that through the grace of the Lord Jesus [1]Christ we shall be saved in the same manner as they."

12Then all the multitude kept silent and listened to Barnabas and Paul declaring how many miracles and **wonders** God had [a]worked through them among the Gentiles. 13And after they had [1]become silent, [a]James answered, saying, "Men *and* brethren, listen to me: 14[a]Simon has declared how God at the first visited the Gentiles to take out of

them a people for His name. 15And with this the words of the prophets *agree, just as it is written:

16 'After[a] this I will return
And will rebuild the tabernacle of
　　David, which has fallen down;
I will rebuild its ruins,
And I will set it up;
17 So that the rest of mankind may seek
　　the LORD,
Even all the Gentiles who are called by
　　My name,
Says the [1]LORD who does all these
　　things.'

18[1]"Known to God from eternity are all His works. 19Therefore [a]I judge that we should not trouble those from among the Gentiles who [b]are turning to God, 20but that we [a]write to them to abstain [b]from things polluted by idols, [c]*from* [1]sexual* immorality, [d]*from* things strangled, and *from* *blood. 21For Moses has had throughout many generations those who preach him in every city, [a]being read in the synagogues every Sabbath."

The Jerusalem Decree

22Then it pleased the apostles and elders, with the whole church, to send chosen men

Cross-references (center column):

2 [a]Gal. 2:1
*See WW at John 14:16.
3 [a]Acts 20:38; 21:5; Rom. 15:24; 1 Cor. 16:6, 11; 2 Cor. 1:16; Titus 3:13; 3 John 6 [b]Acts 14:27; 15:4, 12
5 *See WW at 2 Pet. 2:1.
7 [a]Acts 10:20 *See WW at Mark 1:1.
8 [a]1 Chr. 28:9; Acts 1:24 [b]Acts 2:4; 10:44, 47 [1]bore witness to
9 [a]Rom. 10:12 [b]Acts 10:15, 28 *See WW at Acts 11:12.
10 [a]Matt. 23:4; Gal. 5:1
11 [a]Rom. 3:4; 5:15; 2 Cor. 13:14; [Eph. 2:5–8; Titus 2:11] [1]NU, M omit *Christ*
12 [a]Acts 14:27; 15:3, 4
13 [a]Acts 12:17 [1]stopped speaking
14 [a]Acts 15:7; 2 Pet. 1:1
15 *See WW at Matt. 18:19.
16 [a]Amos 9:11, 12
17 [1]NU *LORD, who makes these things*
18 [1]NU (continuing v. 17) *known from eternity (of old).*
19 [a]Acts 15:28; 21:25 [b]1 Thess. 1:9
20 [a]Acts 21:25 [b]Gen. 35:2; Ex. 20:3, 23; Ezek. 20:30; [1 Cor. 8:1; 10:20, 28]; Rev. 2:14 [c][1 Cor. 6:9]; Gal. 5:19; Eph. 5:3; Col. 3:5; 1 Thess. 4:3; 1 Pet. 4:3 [d]Gen. 9:4; Lev. 3:17; Deut. 12:16; 1 Sam. 14:33 [1]Or *fornication*
*See WW at Matt. 15:19.
• See WW at 1 John 1:7.　21 [a]Acts 13:15, 27; 2 Cor. 3:14

15:12 wonders, *teras;* Strong's #*5059:* Compare "teratology," the science that deals with unexplainable phenomena. *Teras* denotes extraordinary occurrences, supernatural prodigies, omens, portents, unusual manifestations, miraculous incidents portending the future rather than the past, and acts that are so unusual they cause the observer to marvel or be in awe. *Teras* is always in the plural, associated with *sēmeion* (signs). Signs and wonders are a perfect balance for touching man's intellect, emotions, and will.

Footnotes (bottom):

and Judea, so **certain men came down from Judea** to teach the importance of circumcision. They sincerely believed that converts from paganism would weaken the moral standards of the church.

15:2 It is not unusual for Christian leaders to disagree strongly. Acts 15 shows how through the Spirit and open dialogue they are able to resolve their differences.

15:7 Peter refers to his ministry in the house of Cornelius (10:1—11:18).

15:10 To add the Law of Moses to faith is to **test God,** because in effect it means that the sacrificial death of Christ was not quite enough to effect salvation (see Gal. 2:21).

15:12 The irrefutable evidence provided by the demonstrations of the power of the Holy Spirit played a significant role in bringing the Jerusalem Council to its historic decision. See Rom. 15:18, 19; 1 Cor. 2:4; 1 Thess. 1:5.

15:14 There is a subtle play on words here. The root of this

statement is Deut. 14:2, which declares that God will call a people (Israel) out of "all the peoples who are on the face of the earth [the Gentiles]." But James gives new meaning to the long-understood use of these terms. For James, the "people" that God is calling out are Gentiles in contrast to Israel.

15:16, 17 James quotes this OT reference because of its clear prophecy about the salvation of the Gentiles. The rebuilding and restoration of **the tabernacle of David** refers to the building of the church, which in the beginning was composed of Jews, but now included many Gentiles. The church, therefore, is the instrument by which Gentiles may know God. See note on Amos 9:11–15.

15:20 See note on v. 29.

15:22 The Spirit of God brought harmonious agreement among strong-willed leaders in the face of "no small dissension" (v. 2) and "much dispute" (v. 7).

of their own company to Antioch with Paul and Barnabas, *namely,* Judas who was also named [a]Barsabas,[l] and Silas, leading men among the brethren.

23They wrote this *letter* by them:

The apostles, the elders, and the brethren,

To the brethren who are of the Gentiles in Antioch, Syria, and Cilicia:

Greetings.

24 Since we have heard that [a]some who went out from us have *troubled you with words, [b]unsettling your souls, [l]saying, "*You must* be circumcised and keep the law"—to whom we gave no *such* commandment— 25it seemed good to us, being assembled *with one [l]accord, to send chosen men to

you with our beloved Barnabas and Paul, 26[a]men who have risked their lives for the name of our Lord Jesus Christ. 27We have therefore sent Judas and Silas, who will also report the same things by word of mouth. 28For it seemed good to the Holy Spirit, and to us, to lay upon you no greater burden than these necessary things: 29[a]that you abstain from things offered to idols, [b]from blood, from things strangled, and from [c]sexual[l] immorality. If you keep yourselves from these, you will do well.

Farewell.

Continuing Ministry in Syria

30So when they were sent off, they came to Antioch; and when they had gathered the

Center column references:

22 [a]Acts 1:23
[l]NU, M Barsab-bas
24 [a]Acts 15:1; Gal. 2:4; 5:12; Titus 1:10, 11
[b]Gal. 1:7; 5:10
[l]NU omits saying, "You must be circumcised and keep the law"
*See WW at Luke 24:38.
25 [l]purpose or mind
*See WW at Acts 2:1.
26 [a]Acts 13:50; 14:19; 1 Cor. 15:30; 2 Cor. 11:23–26
29 [a]Acts 15:20; 21:25; Rev. 2:14, 20 [b]Lev. 17:14 [c]1 Cor. 5:1; 6:18; 7:2; Col. 3:5; 1 Thess. 4:3
[l]Or fornication

15:23 The salutation of the letter affirms the unity of the leadership of the church.

15:28 It seemed good to the Holy Spirit, and to us: An earnest and common desire to know the mind of God leads to unanimity. A church possessing an awareness of the guidance of the Holy Spirit (see 10:19, 20; 13:2, 3) need not be unassisted in pursuing its decisions.

15:29 Things offered to idols was meat that had been offered as a sacrifice and was later sold in the market as "used" meat (see 1 Cor. 8). It appears that the early church is substituting three "new" laws for the "old" laws of Judaism. In view of the clear teaching on grace in this chapter (Acts 15:11), these cannot be seen as requirements for salvation. Instead, they represent a basic separation from glaring paganism and its practices, particularly offensive to Jewish scruples.

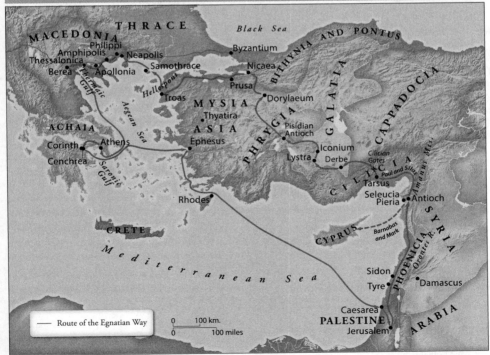

PAUL GOES TO GREECE (THE SECOND MISSIONARY JOURNEY, ACTS 15:39—18:22)

Starting from Jerusalem, Paul took Silas to visit again the churches of Galatia. Young Timothy joined them in Lystra. Then they went to Macedonia and Achaia, present-day Greece. On this journey the Philippian jailer was saved, the Bereans "searched the Scriptures daily" (Acts 17:11), and Paul preached at the Areopagus in Athens and then settled in Corinth for a year and a half.

multitude together, they delivered the letter. 31When they had read it, they rejoiced over its encouragement. 32Now Judas and Silas, themselves being ^aprophets also, ^bexhorted and strengthened the brethren with many words. 33And after they had stayed *there* for a time, they were ^asent back with greetings from the brethren to ^lthe apostles.

34^lHowever, it seemed good to Silas to remain there. 35^aPaul and Barnabas also remained in Antioch, teaching and preaching the word of the Lord, with many others also.

Division over John Mark

36Then after some days Paul said to Barnabas, "Let us now go back and visit our brethren in every city where we have preached the word of the Lord, *and see* how they are doing." 37Now Barnabas ^lwas determined to take with them ^aJohn called Mark. 38But Paul insisted that they should not take with them ^athe one who had departed from them in Pamphylia, and had not gone with them to the work. 39Then the contention became so sharp that they parted from one another. And so Barnabas took Mark and sailed to ^aCyprus; 40but Paul chose Silas and departed, ^abeing ^lcommended by the brethren to the grace of God. 41And he went through Syria and Cilicia, ^astrengthening the churches.

Timothy Joins Paul and Silas

③ **16** Then he came to ^aDerbe and Lystra. And behold, a certain disciple was there, ^bnamed Timothy, ^c*the* son of a certain Jewish woman who believed, but his father *was* Greek. 2He was well spoken of by the brethren who were at Lystra and Iconium. 3Paul wanted to have him go on with him. And he ^atook *him* and circumcised him because of the Jews who were in that region, for they all knew that his father was Greek. 4And as they went through the cities, they delivered to them the ^adecrees to keep, ^bwhich were determined by the

apostles and elders at Jerusalem. 5^aSo the churches were *strengthened in the faith, and *increased in number daily.

The Macedonian Call

6Now when they had gone through Phrygia and the region of ^aGalatia, they were forbidden by the Holy Spirit to preach the *word in ^lAsia. 7After they had come to Mysia, they tried to go into Bithynia, but the ^lSpirit did not permit them. 8So passing by Mysia, they ^acame down to Troas. 9And a vision appeared to Paul in the night. A ^aman of Macedonia stood and pleaded with him, saying, "Come over to Macedonia and help us." 10Now after he had seen the vision, immediately we sought to go ^ato Macedonia, concluding that the Lord had called us to preach the gospel to them.

Lydia Baptized at Philippi

11Therefore, sailing from Troas, we ran a straight course to Samothrace, and the next *day* came to Neapolis, 12and from there to ^aPhilippi, which is the ^lforemost city of that part of Macedonia, a colony. And we were staying in that city for some days. 13And on the Sabbath day we went out of the city to the riverside, where prayer was customarily made; and we sat down and spoke to the women who met *there*. 14Now a certain woman named Lydia heard *us*. She was a seller of purple from the city of ^aThyatira, who worshiped God. ^bThe Lord *opened her heart to heed the things spoken by Paul. 15And when she and her household were baptized, she begged *us*, saying, "If you have judged me to be faithful to the Lord, come to my house and stay." So ^ashe persuaded us.

Paul and Silas Imprisoned

16Now it happened, as we went to prayer, that a certain slave girl ^apossessed with a

32 ^aActs 11:27; 1 Cor. 12:28; Eph. 4:11; Rev. 18:20 ^bActs 14:22; 18:23
33 ^aMark 5:34; Acts 16:36; 1 Cor. 16:11; Heb. 11:31 ^lNU those who had sent them
34 ^lNU, M omit v. 34.
35 ^aActs 13:1
37 ^aActs 12:12, 25; Col. 4:10; 2 Tim. 4:11; Philem. 24 ^lresolved
38 ^aActs 13:13
39 ^aActs 4:36; 13:4
40 ^aActs 11:23; 14:26 ^lcommitted
41 ^aActs 16:5

CHAPTER 16
1 ^aActs 14:6 ^bActs 19:22; Rom. 16:21; 1 Cor. 4:17; 16:10; Phil. 1:1; 2:19; 1 Thess. 3:2; 2 Tim. 1:2 ^c2 Tim. 1:5; 3:15
3 ^a[1 Cor. 9:20; Gal. 2:3; 5:2]
4 ^aActs 15:19–21 ^bActs 15:28, 29
5 ^aActs 2:47; 15:41
*See WW at Col. 2:5. • See WW at Matt. 25:29.
6 ^aActs 18:23; Gal. 1:1, 2 ^lThe Roman province of Asia
*See WW at Acts 19:20.
7 ^lNU adds of Jesus
8 ^aActs 16:11; 20:5; 2 Cor. 2:12; 2 Tim. 4:13
9 ^aActs 10:30
10 ^a2 Cor. 2:13
12 ^aActs 20:6; Phil. 1:1; 1 Thess. 2:2 ^lLit. first
14 ^aRev. 1:11; 2:18, 24 ^bLuke 24:45
*See WW at Luke 24:31.
15 ^aGen. 19:3;

33:11; Judg. 19:21; Luke 24:29; [Heb. 13:2] **16** ^aLev. 19:31; 20:6, 27; Deut. 18:11; 1 Sam. 28:3, 7; 2 Kin. 21:6; 1 Chr. 10:13; Is. 8:19

15:31 Legalism is always accompanied by fear and bondage; the message of grace is "good news," and brings liberty and joy.

15:36–41 The contention (v. 39) between **Paul** and **Barnabas** arose over a difference of opinion concerning the inclusion of **Mark** on the mission team. Paul considered Mark's departure on the previous journey a desertion (see 13:13). Paul later changed his mind about John Mark (see Col. 4:10). Unfortunately, painful divisions in the body of Christ do occur, but God can turn such things to good. In the case of Paul and Barnabas, there are now *two* missionary teams instead of one (vv. 39, 40). This is the beginning of Paul's next trip abroad. See map of Paul's second journey.

16:1–5 See section 3 of Truth in Action at the end of Acts.

16:1 Timothy becomes one of Paul's disciples and later is the recipient of 1 and 2 Tim.

16:3 Paul, the chief spokesman of salvation by grace alone, had the half-Jewish Timothy **circumcised** so that he could take him into the Jewish synagogues. This was not compromise; it was

simple Christian courtesy. It was a mature recognition that social, cultural, and even religious differences should never become more important issues than the simple message of salvation in Christ. See 1 Cor. 9:19–23.

16:7 Luke does not indicate how **the Spirit** communicated His will to the missionaries. It may have been through inner prompting, prophetic utterance, or external circumstances.

16:9 Macedonia is northern Greece, including the cities of Philippi and Thessalonica, to which Paul later addressed three of his epistles.

16:11 This verse begins the "we" sections of Acts, indicating that Luke has joined the mission team and is now giving a firsthand report.

16:13 Since Jewish law required the establishment of a synagogue when there was a population of at least 10 men in a community, the absence of a synagogue in Philippi indicates a small Jewish population.

spirit of divination met us, who brought her masters *b*much profit by fortune-telling. 17This girl followed Paul and us, and cried out, saying, "These men are the *servants of the Most High God, who proclaim to us the way of salvation." 18And this she did for many days.

But Paul, *a*greatly *l*annoyed, turned and said to the spirit, "I command you in the name of Jesus Christ to come out of her." *b*And he came out that very hour. 19But *a*when her masters saw that their hope of profit was gone, they seized Paul and Silas and *b*dragged *them* into the marketplace to the authorities.

20And they brought them to the magistrates, and said, "These men, being Jews, *a*exceedingly trouble our city; 21and they teach customs which are not lawful for us, being Romans, to receive or observe." 22Then the multitude rose up together against them; and the magistrates tore off their clothes *a*and commanded *them* to be beaten with rods. 23And when they had laid many stripes on them, they threw *them* into prison, commanding the jailer to keep them securely. 24Having received such a **charge**, he put them into the inner prison and fastened their feet in the stocks.

The Philippian Jailer Saved

25But at midnight Paul and Silas were praying and singing hymns to God, and the

WORD ⚔ WEALTH

16:24 charge, *parangelia*; Strong's *#3852*: A chain-of-command word, denoting a general order, instruction, command, precept, or direction. It is used in a way that makes the word self-explanatory. The prison authorities charge the jailer to imprison Paul and Silas (v. 24). The apostles were given a charge not to preach by the authorities at Jerusalem (5:28). Paul gives a charge to the Thessalonians (1 Thess. 4:2). *Parangelia* is the charge Paul gave to Timothy (1 Tim. 1:5, 18).

prisoners were listening to them. 26*a*Suddenly there was a great earthquake, so that the foundations of the prison were shaken; and immediately *b*all the doors were opened and everyone's chains were loosed. 27And the keeper of the prison, awaking from sleep and seeing the prison doors open, supposing the prisoners had fled, drew his sword and was about to kill himself. 28But Paul called with a loud voice, saying, "Do yourself no harm, for we are all here."

29Then he called for a light, ran in, and fell down trembling before Paul and Silas. 30And he brought them out and said, *a*"Sirs, what must I do to be saved?"

31So they said, *a*"Believe* on the Lord Jesus Christ, and you will be *saved, you and your household." 32Then they spoke the word of the Lord to him and to all who were in his house. 33And he took them the same hour of the night and washed *their* stripes. And immediately he and all his *family* were baptized. 34Now when he had brought them into his house, *a*he set food before them; and he rejoiced, having believed in God with all his household.

Paul Refuses to Depart Secretly

35And when it was day, the magistrates sent the *l*officers, saying, "Let those men go."

36So the keeper of the prison reported these words to Paul, saying, "The magistrates have sent to let you go. Now therefore depart, and go in peace."

37But Paul said to them, "They have beaten us openly, uncondemned *a*Romans, *and* have thrown *us* into prison. And now do they put us out secretly? No indeed! Let them come themselves and get us out."

38And the officers told these words to the magistrates, and they were *afraid when they heard that they were Romans. 39Then they came and pleaded with them and brought *them* out, and *a*asked *them* to depart from the city. 40So they went out of

Cross references (center column):

16 *b*Acts 19:24
17 *See WW at Rev. 19:5.
18 *a*Mark 1:25, 34 *b*Mark 16:17 *l*distressed
19 *a*Acts 16:16; 19:25, 26 *b*Matt. 10:18
20 *a*1 Kin. 18:17; Acts 17:8
22 *a*2 Cor. 6:5; 11:23, 25; 1 Thess. 2:2
26 *a*Acts 4:31 *b*Acts 5:19; 12:7, 10
30 *a*Luke 3:10; Acts 2:37; 9:6; 22:10
31 *a*[John 3:16, 36; 6:47; Acts 13:38, 39; Rom. 10:9–11; 1 John 5:10] *See WW at Rom. 10:9. • *See WW at Matt. 9:22.
34 *a*Matt. 5:4; Luke 5:29; 19:6
35 *l*lictors, lit. rod bearers
37 *a*Acts 22:25–29
38 *See WW at Matt. 10:26.
39 *a*Matt. 8:34

16:16 The slave girl had **a spirit of divination,** or literally, "a spirit, a python," characterizing her as one inspired by Apollo, the god worshiped at Pytho (Delphi).

16:17 The demon in the slave girl spoke the truth, but mockingly. See Mark 1:24, 25.

16:18 Why Paul delayed to cast out the demon is uncertain. Perhaps he was aware of the peril to which the exorcism would expose the mission team.

16:19–21 This was Paul's first clash with Roman officials. The new Christian sect was not a threat to the peace of Rome. The charges here were false, and Paul and Silas were completely exonerated by Roman justice (vv. 34–39).

16:25 Paul and Silas rejoiced in the face of their terrible circumstances. As he later wrote back to the church he had planted in this very city of Philippi, Paul commanded from another prison cell, "Rejoice in the Lord always" (Phil. 4:4).

16:26 This is the power of praise in action, although it must be remembered that Paul was in prison at other times and this kind of spectacular event did not occur.

16:30, 31 Luke was not only recording an important moment in early church history; he was recording a universal question and the precise answer to that question. **You and your household** suggests that God works in family units (see Ex. 12:3). Though a wonderful promise, it is not a guaranteed promise that all loved ones will be saved. Each must still respond individually to Jesus.

16:37 This is the first of several instances where Paul appeals to his Roman citizenship. A relatively small proportion of the population of the Roman Empire held citizenship, a rare and valuable status (22:27, 28); and Roman law guaranteed the legal rights of its official citizens, including the right to a fair trial (22:25, 26; 25:16). Paul's insistence on fair treatment is to turn the tables on the lies of his accusers (v. 21).

WORD | WEALTH

17:3 suffer, *paschō;* Strong's *#3958:* Compare "passion," "passive," "pathos." Being acted upon in a certain way, to experience ill-treatment, roughness, violence, or outrage, to endure suffering, and to undergo evils from without. *Paschō* asks the painful question, "What is happening to me?" Of the 42 times it appears, it is mostly used of Christ's suffering for us.

the prison [a]and entered *the house of* Lydia; and when they had seen the brethren, they encouraged them and departed.

Preaching Christ at Thessalonica

17 Now when they had passed through Amphipolis and Apollonia, they came to [a]Thessalonica, where there was a synagogue of the Jews. [2]Then Paul, as his custom was, [a]went in to them, and for three Sabbaths [b]reasoned with them from the Scriptures, [3]explaining and demonstrating [a]that the Christ had to **suffer** and rise again from the dead, and *saying,* "This Jesus whom I preach to you is the Christ." [4a]And some of them were persuaded; and a great multitude of the devout Greeks, and not a few of the leading women, joined Paul and [b]Silas.

Assault on Jason's House

[5]But the Jews [1]who were not persuaded, [2]becoming [a]envious,* took some of the evil men from the marketplace, and gathering a mob, set all the city in an uproar and attacked the house of [b]Jason, and sought to bring them out to the people. [6]But when they did not find them, they dragged Jason and some brethren to the rulers of the city, crying out, [a]"These who have turned the world upside down have come here too. [7]Jason has [1]harbored them, and these are all acting contrary to the decrees of Caesar, [a]saying there is another king—Jesus." [8]And they *troubled the crowd and the rulers of the city when they heard these things. [9]So when they had taken security from Jason and the rest, they let them go.

Ministering at Berea

[10]Then [a]the brethren immediately sent Paul and Silas away by night to Berea. When they arrived, they went into the synagogue of the Jews. [11]These were more [1]fair-minded

---

40 [a]Acts 16:14

CHAPTER 17
1 [a]Acts 17:11, 13; 20:4; 27:2; Phil. 4:16; 1 Thess. 1:1; 2 Thess. 1:1; 2 Tim. 4:10
2 [a]Luke 4:16; Acts 9:20; 13:5, 14; 14:1; 16:13; 19:8
[b]1 Thess. 2:1–16
3 [a]Luke 24:26, 46; Acts 18:5, 28; Gal. 3:1
[b]Acts 15:22, 27, 32, 40
5 [a]Acts 13:45
[b]Acts 17:6, 7, 9; Rom. 16:21
[1]NU omits *who were not persuaded* [2]M omits *becoming envious*
*See WW at 1 Cor. 14:1.
6 [a][Acts 16:20]
7 [a]Luke 23:2; John 19:12; 1 Pet. 2:13
[1]welcomed
8 *See WW at Luke 24:38.
10 [a]Acts 9:25; 17:14
11 [1]Lit. noble

[a]Is. 34:16; Luke 16:29; John 5:39
14 [a]Matt. 10:23
*See WW at Matt. 24:13.
15 [a]Acts 18:5
16 [a]2 Pet. 2:8
[1]full of idols

KINGDOM | DYNAMICS

17:6 Guidelines Amid a Visitation, REVIVAL. So explosive was the revival in Acts, it was as if the world had turned "upside down." A visitation of God's Spirit puts leadership in a role requiring wisdom in "handling" such explosiveness. To see His purpose fully accomplished, these guidelines may help: (1) *Follow the life of the Holy Spirit.* If we respond to the revival in fear (quenching the Spirit) or presumption (seizing initiative God has not given us), we grieve the Holy Spirit (see Eph. 4:30; 5:18; 1 Thess. 5:19). (2) *Resolve not to "control" the revival.* Seek God for discernment between "leading" and "restricting"; monitor the visitation, but stay submitted to Him. Give wise stewardship to the gracious move of the Spirit (see 1 Cor. 4:1, 2; James 4:7; 1 Pet. 2:21). (3) *Seek the counsel of gifted ministries,* each submitting to and complementing the other as God has designed His church to work together (see Prov. 11:14; 1 Cor. 12:1–28; 14:32; Eph. 4:11, 12; 1 Thess. 5:11). (4) *Always complement the experiential side of the visitation with the consistent, systematic teaching of the Word of God* (see Luke 24:27; Acts 17:11; Eph. 6:17; Heb. 4:12). (5) *Always keep the focus of the revival on God, not "things that happen."* In a genuine move of God, people will need to be led to worship God and glorify Him as the Initiator and Sustainer of such blessing and the Source of wisdom and power to walk wisely in it. (John 17:4/Prov. 18:19) G.F.

than those in Thessalonica, in that they received the word with all readiness, and [a]searched the Scriptures daily *to find out* whether these things were so. [12]Therefore many of them believed, and also not a few of the Greeks, prominent women as well as men. [13]But when the Jews from Thessalonica learned that the word of God was preached by Paul at Berea, they came there also and stirred up the crowds. [14a]Then immediately the brethren sent Paul away, to go to the sea; but both Silas and Timothy *remained there. [15]So those who conducted Paul brought him to Athens; and [a]receiving a command for Silas and Timothy to come to him with all speed, they departed.

The Philosophers at Athens

[16]Now while Paul waited for them at Athens, [a]his spirit was provoked within him when he saw that the city was [1]given over to idols. [17]Therefore he reasoned in the synagogue with the Jews and with the

---

17:2 Paul usually began his ministry in a new city by going into the Jewish synagogue, which offered a relatively open forum for Jews to teach and address current issues. Even though Paul was persecuted by his brethren, the Jews, he never lost his burden for their souls (see Rom. 9:1–5).

17:11 These Jews did not have closed minds; **they received the word with all readiness.** Nor were they gullible; they **searched the Scriptures daily.**

WORD WEALTH

17:18 babbler, *spermologos;* Strong's #4691: Athenian slang for: (1) a bird that picks up seeds; (2) men lounging around the marketplace, making a living by picking up whatever falls from the loads of merchandise; (3) a babbler, chatterer, or gossip retailing bits and pieces of misinformation; and (4) a pseudo-intellectual who insists on spouting off. Tragically, the super-intellectuals on Mars' Hill failed to see in Paul all the necessary ingredients for being a truth bringer.

Gentile worshipers, and in the marketplace daily with those who happened to be there. 18ʲThen certain Epicurean and Stoic philosophers encountered him. And some said, "What does this ²**babbler** want to say?"

Others said, "He seems to be a proclaimer of foreign gods," because he preached to them ᵃJesus and the resurrection.

19And they took him and brought him to the ʲAreopagus, saying, "May we know what this *new doctrine *is* of which you speak? 20For you are bringing some strange things to our ears. Therefore we want to know what these things mean." 21For all the Athenians and the foreigners who were there spent their time in nothing else but either to tell or to hear some new thing.

Addressing the Areopagus

22Then Paul stood in the midst of the ʲAreopagus and said, "Men of Athens, I perceive that in all things you are very religious; 23for as I was passing through and considering the objects of your worship, I even found an altar with this inscription:

TO THE UNKNOWN GOD.

Therefore, the One whom you worship without knowing, Him I proclaim to you: 24ᵃGod, who made the world and everything in it, since He is ᵇLord of heaven and earth, ᶜdoes not dwell in temples made with hands. 25Nor is He worshiped with men's

---

Center column references

18 ᵃ1 Cor. 15:12
ʲNU, M add
also ²Lit. *seed
picker,* an idler
who makes a
living picking
up scraps
19 ʲLit. *Hill of
Ares,* or *Mars'
Hill*
*See WW at
2 Cor. 5:17.
22 ʲLit. *Hill of
Ares,* or *Mars'
Hill*
24 ᵃIs. 42:5;
Acts 14:15
ᵇDeut. 10:14;
Ps. 115:16;
Matt. 11:25
ᶜ1 Kin. 8:27;
Acts 7:48–50

25 ᵃGen. 2:7;
Is. 42:5; Dan.
5:23
26 ᵃDeut. 32:8;
Job 12:23;
Dan. 4:35 ʲNU
omits *blood*
27 ᵃ[Rom. 1:20]
ᵇDeut. 4:7;
Ps. 139:7, 10;
Jer. 23:23, 24;
[Acts 14:17]
28 ᵃ[Col. 1:17;
Heb. 1:3]
ᵇTitus 1:12
29 ᵃPs. 115:4–7;
Is. 40:18, 19;
Rom. 1:23
30 ᵃActs 14:16;
[Rom. 3:25]
ᵇLuke 24:47;
Acts 26:20;
[Titus 2:11,
12]; 1 Pet.
1:14; 4:3
*See WW at
Matt. 3:2.
31 ᵃPs. 9:8;
96:13; 98:9;
John 5:22, 27;
Acts 10:42;
Rom. 2:16
ᵇActs 2:24

KINGDOM DYNAMICS

17:26–29 The Unity of the Human Race, HUMAN WORTH/DIVINE DESTINY. It was never God's intention to have humanity—the jewel of creation—as divided as we are. The essence of the Holy Trinity is best appreciated when we consider both the *uniqueness* of Father, Son, and Holy Spirit and the *unity* of Father, Son, and Holy Spirit. While every human being is unique, God calls us to take on His character and unite with others. We are united by blood, for He made us from one blood. He also redeemed us with one blood. We are also united in our seeking of God and in the hope we pursue. Let us work toward greater love and unity based on our common origin and our common destiny. (Luke 10:33/ Eph. 2:1–10) S.R.

hands, as though He needed anything, since He ᵃgives to all life, breath, and all things. 26And He has made from one ʲblood every nation of men to dwell on all the face of the earth, and has determined their preappointed times and ᵃthe boundaries of their dwellings, 27ᵃso that they should seek the Lord, in the hope that they might grope for Him and find Him, ᵇthough He is not far from each one of us; 28for ᵃin Him we live and move and have our being, ᵇas also some of your own poets have said, 'For we are also His offspring.' 29Therefore, since we are the offspring of God, ᵃwe ought not to think that the Divine Nature is like gold or silver or stone, something shaped by art and man's devising. 30Truly, ᵃthese times of ignorance God overlooked, but ᵇnow commands all men everywhere to *repent, 31because He has appointed a day on which ᵃHe will judge the world in righteousness by the Man whom He has ordained. He has given assurance of this to all by ᵇraising Him from the dead."

32And when they heard of the resurrection of the dead, some mocked, while others said, "We will hear you again on this *matter.* 33So Paul departed from among

---

17:18 The people of the Roman Empire were characterized by a great diversity of religious belief. Epicureanism (seeking tranquility as the highest good) and Stoicism (being free from passion and passively accepting everything in life as inevitable, impersonal fate) were popular philosophies. Polytheism (the belief in multiple gods) was rampant: "The city was given over to idols" (v. 16). These philosophers actually thought that Paul was propagating a religion of two new gods: **Jesus and the resurrection.** Others, however, accused Paul of being a **babbler.** The word originally described one who picked up scraps in the marketplace. Later, it designated one who picked up scraps of learning here and there and peddled them.

17:19 The **Areopagus**, or "Hill of Ares" (Roman, "of Mars"), was an open forum for philosophical debate, and was located southwest of the Parthenon on the Acropolis.

17:22 Athens was the religious center of the Greco-Roman world.

There were more statues of gods in Athens than in all the rest of Greece put together. The phrase **very religious** is not a compliment, but a statement of fact. It could be understood as "somewhat superstitious."

17:23 In spite of their religiosity, the Athenians were ignorant of the true God.

17:24–31 Paul did not quote from the Hebrew Scriptures, which were unfamiliar to his Greek audience. For reasons Luke does not explain, results here were meager (v. 34)—no baptisms, no new church, and no letter to the Athenians in the NT—in contrast to other places where the power of God was the front line of his ministry.

17:32 To the Greeks the idea of the resurrection of the dead was ridiculous, because they believed that death was a release of the soul from the prison of the body.

them. [34]However, some men joined him and believed, among them Dionysius the Areopagite, a woman named Damaris, and others with them.

Ministering at Corinth

18 After these things Paul departed from Athens and went to Corinth. [2]And he found a certain Jew named [a]Aquila, born in Pontus, who had recently come from Italy with his wife Priscilla (because Claudius had commanded all the Jews to depart from Rome); and he came to them. [3]So, because he was of the same trade, he stayed with them [a]and worked; for by occupation they were tentmakers. [4][a]And he reasoned in the synagogue every Sabbath, and persuaded both Jews and Greeks.

[5][a]When Silas and Timothy had come from Macedonia, Paul was [b]compelled* [1]by the Spirit, and testified to the Jews *that* Jesus *is* the Christ. [6]But [a]when they opposed him and blasphemed, [b]he shook *his* garments and said to them, [c]"Your blood *be* upon your *own* heads; [d]I *am* clean. [e]From now on I will go to the Gentiles." [7]And he departed from there and entered the house of a certain *man* named [1]Justus, *one* who worshiped God, whose house was next door to the synagogue. [8][a]Then Crispus, the ruler of the synagogue, believed on the Lord with all his household. And many of the Corinthians, hearing, believed and were baptized.

[9]Now [a]the Lord spoke to Paul in the night by a vision, "Do not be afraid, but speak, and do not keep silent; [10][a]for I am with you, and no one will attack you to hurt you; for I have many people in this city." [11]And he continued *there* a year and six months, teaching the word of God among them.

[12]When Gallio was proconsul of Achaia, the Jews *with one accord rose up against Paul and brought him to the [1]judgment* seat, [13]saying, "This *fellow* persuades men to worship God contrary to the law."

[14]And when Paul was about to open *his* mouth, Gallio said to the Jews, "If it were a matter of wrongdoing or wicked crimes,

O Jews, there would be reason why I should *bear with you. [15]But if it is a [a]question of words and names and your own law, look *to it* yourselves; for I do not want to be a judge of such *matters.*" [16]And he drove them from the *judgment seat. [17]Then [1]all the Greeks took [a]Sosthenes, the ruler of the synagogue, and beat *him* before the judgment seat. But Gallio took no notice of these things.

Paul Returns to Antioch

[18]So Paul still remained [1]a good while. Then he took *leave of the brethren and sailed for Syria, and Priscilla and Aquila *were* with him. [a]He had *his* hair cut off at [b]Cenchrea, for he had taken a vow. [19]And he came to Ephesus, and left them there; but he himself entered the synagogue and reasoned with the Jews. [20]When they asked *him* to stay a longer time with them, he did not consent, [21]but took leave of them, saying, [a]"I[1] must by all means keep this coming feast in Jerusalem; but I will return again to you, [b]God willing." And he sailed from Ephesus.

[22]And when he had landed at [a]Caesarea, and [1]gone up and greeted the church, he went down to Antioch. [23]After he had spent some time *there,* he departed and went over the region of [a]Galatia and Phrygia [1]in order, [b]strengthening all the disciples.

Ministry of Apollos

[24][a]Now a certain Jew named Apollos, born at Alexandria, an eloquent man *and *mighty in the *Scriptures, came to Ephesus. [25]This man had been instructed in the way of the Lord; and being [a]fervent in spirit, he spoke and taught accurately the things of the Lord, [b]though he knew only the baptism of John. [26]So he began to speak boldly in the synagogue. When Aquila and Priscilla heard him, they took him aside and explained to him the way of God more accurately. [27]And when he desired to cross to Achaia, the brethren wrote, exhorting

CHAPTER 18
2 [a]Rom. 16:3; 1 Cor. 16:19; 2 Tim. 4:19
3 [a]Acts 20:34; 1 Cor. 4:12; 9:14; 2 Cor. 11:7; 12:13; 1 Thess. 2:9; 4:11; 2 Thess. 3:8
4 [a]Acts 17:2
5 [a]Acts 17:14, 15 [b]Acts 18:28 [1]Or *in his spirit or in the Spirit* *See WW at 2 Cor. 5:14.
6 [a]Acts 13:45 [b]Neh. 5:13; Matt. 10:14; Acts 13:51 [c]Lev. 20:9, 11, 12; 2 Sam. 1:16; 1 Kin. 2:33; Ezek. 18:13; 33:4, 6, 8; Matt. 27:25; Acts 20:26 [d][Ezek. 3:18, 19] [e]Acts 13:46–48; 28:28
7 [1]NU *Titius Justus*
8 [a]1 Cor. 1:14
9 [a]Acts 23:11
10 [a]Jer. 1:18, 19
12 [1]Gr. *bema* *See WW at Acts 2:1. • See WW at Matt. 27:19.
14 *See WW at 2 Thess. 1:4.
15 [a]Acts 23:29; 25:19
16 *See WW at Matt. 27:19.
17 [a]1 Cor. 1:1 [1]NU *they all*
18 [a]Num. 6:2, 5, 9, 18; Acts 21:24 [b]Rom. 16:1 [1]Lit. *many days* *See WW at Luke 14:33.
21 [a]Acts 19:21; 20:16 [b]1 Cor. 4:19; Heb. 6:3; James 4:15 [1]NU omits *I must by all means keep this coming feast in Jerusalem*
22 [a]Acts 8:40 [1]To Jerusalem
23 [a]Gal. 1:2 [b]Acts 14:22; 15:32, 41 [1]successively
24 [a]Acts 19:1; 1 Cor. 1:12; 3:4; 16:12; Titus 3:13 *See WW at Matt.
19:26. • See WW at John 5:39. 25 [a]Rom. 12:11 [b][Matt. 3:1–11; Mark 1:7, 8; Luke 3:16, 17; 7:29; John 1:26, 33]; Acts 19:3

18:2 Claudius banished Jews from Rome in A.D. 49.

18:3 Paul, the brilliant and gifted apostle of Christ, was not afraid of manual labor. His vocation was tentmaking, or possibly leatherwork. In ancient Judaism it was improper for a rabbi to receive money for his teaching.

18:4 Greeks in the synagogue were proselytes, converts to Judaism.

18:6 See note on 13:51. **From now on I will go to the Gentiles** must refer only to Corinth, because later Paul goes back to the synagogue in other cities (see 18:19; 19:8).

18:12 Gallio was the brother of the famous Roman orator, Seneca. He became governor of Achaia in A.D. 52.

18:18 This **vow** is difficult to identify. A Nazirite vow could not be

undertaken outside of Judea, so this was probably some private vow of thanksgiving for the fulfillment of God's promise to him in vv. 9, 10 and his protection in Corinth.

18:22 Greeted the church in Jerusalem.

18:23 This verse is the quiet beginning of Paul's third international trip. See map of Paul's third journey.

18:24 The references Paul makes to Apollos in 1 Cor. 1:12; 3:4 indicate that later he became well known to the Corinthian church.

18:26 Explained . . . more accurately may refer to Apollos's unexpanded view of the Holy Spirit's ministry, which Paul will discover among the Ephesians to whom Apollos had ministered (v. 24; 19:1, 2). **Priscilla** apparently occupies the office of pastor-teacher, along with her husband, **Aquila.** See notes on Rom. 16:3, 4; 16:5.

WORD ✦ WEALTH

18:25 fervent, *zeō*; Strong's #2204: Compare "zeal," "zeolite," or "seethe." Living fervor, fiery hot, full of burning zeal. It is the opposite of dignified, cold, and unemotional. In a Christian context it signifies a high spiritual temperature, inflamed by the Holy Spirit. Apollos was a complete man, articulate in Scripture, and full of spiritual fervency.

the disciples to receive him; and when he arrived, ᵃhe greatly helped those who had believed through grace; 28for he vigorously refuted the Jews publicly, ᵃshowing from the Scriptures that Jesus is the Christ.

Paul at Ephesus

19 And it happened, while ᵃApollos was at Corinth, that Paul, having passed through ᵇthe upper regions, came

27 ᵃ1 Cor. 3:6
28 ᵃActs 9:22; 17:3; 18:5

CHAPTER 19
1 ᵃ1 Cor. 1:12; 3:5, 6; Titus 3:13 ᵇActs 18:23

2 ᵃ1 Sam. 3:7; Acts 8:16
3 ᵃLuke 7:29; Acts 18:25
4 ᵃMatt. 3:11; Mark 1:4, 7, 8; Luke 3:16; [John 1:15, 26, 27]; Acts 13:24
5 ᵃMatt. 28:19; Acts 8:12, 16; 10:48
6 ᵃActs 6:6; 8:17 ᵇMark 16:17; Acts 2:4; 10:46
8 ᵃActs 17:2; 18:4

to Ephesus. And finding some disciples 2he said to them, "Did you receive the Holy Spirit when you believed?"

So they said to him, ᵃ"We have not so much as heard whether there is a Holy Spirit."

3And he said to them, "Into what then were you baptized?"

So they said, ᵃ"Into John's baptism."

4Then Paul said, ᵃ"John indeed baptized with a baptism of repentance, saying to the people that they should believe on Him who would come after him, that is, on Christ Jesus."

5When they heard *this,* they were baptized ᵃin the name of the Lord Jesus. 6And when Paul had ᵃlaid hands on them, the Holy Spirit came upon them, and ᵇthey spoke with tongues and prophesied. 7Now the men were about twelve in all.

8ᵃAnd he went into the synagogue and

19:1–7 Upon arriving in Ephesus, Paul finds a group of **disciples** (a clear indication that they are true, baptized Christians) whose knowledge about **the Holy Spirit** is defective. Their teachers knew some basics of Christianity from contact with John the Baptist, but they were apparently unaware of the developments of Pentecost. Therefore, these disciples had only been baptized **into John's baptism.** This indicates that their conversion experience was accompanied by the knowledge that a fuller experience with the Holy Spirit would come (Matt. 3:11), but without the realization that it had come (Acts 2:1–4). Paul remedies this by rebaptizing them in water (the only such account in the NT) and by leading them into a fuller experience with the Holy Spirit (v. 6). An obvious parallel to the Day of Pentecost, the Spirit's fullness is displayed by their speaking in tongues and prophesying. See note on 2:4.

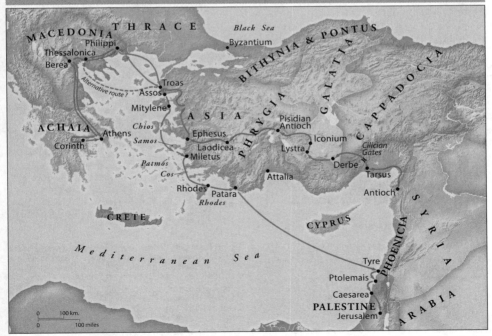

ASIA AND GREECE REVISITED (PAUL'S THIRD MISSIONARY JOURNEY, ACTS 18:23 — 21:16)

Paul visited the churches of Galatia for a third time, and then settled in Ephesus for more than two years. Upon leaving Ephesus, Paul traveled again to Macedonia and Achaia (Greece) for a three-month stay. He returned to Asia by way of Macedonia. On his third journey Paul wrote 1 Corinthians from Ephesus, 2 Corinthians from Macedonia, and the letter to the Romans from Corinth.

KINGDOM DYNAMICS

19:6 Water Baptism and Holy Spirit Baptism, HOLY SPIRIT FULLNESS. As in Samaria with Peter and John, here Paul showed the same concern over those in Ephesus. Drawing the distinction between water baptism and receiving the Holy Spirit, he "laid hands on them." When "the Holy Spirit came upon them," similar results attended their experience, just as other miracle signs in Acts. Most significantly, just as in Jerusalem, before long the entire city was awakened to the message of Jesus and the Resurrection (v. 10). This is the greatest sign of Holy Spirit fullness: He enables believers in a bold, penetrating witness that impacts cultures alien to God's Word of truth (v. 20). (Acts 10:44–48/ 1 Cor. 12:10) S.G.B.

spoke boldly for three months, reasoning and *persuading [b]concerning the things of the kingdom of God. 9But [a]when some were hardened and did not believe, but spoke evil [b]of the Way before the multitude, he departed from them and withdrew the disciples, reasoning daily in the school of Tyrannus. 10And [a]this continued for two years, so that all who dwelt in Asia heard the word of the Lord Jesus, both Jews and Greeks.

Miracles Glorify Christ

11Now [a]God worked unusual miracles by the hands of Paul, 12[a]so that even handkerchiefs or aprons were brought from his body to the sick, and the diseases left them and the evil spirits went out of them. 13[a]Then some of the itinerant Jewish exorcists [b]took it upon themselves to call the name of the Lord Jesus over those who had evil spirits, saying, 1"We 2exorcise you by the Jesus whom Paul [c]preaches." 14Also there were seven sons of Sceva, a Jewish chief priest, who did so.

15And the evil spirit answered and said, "Jesus I know, and Paul I know; but who are you?"

16Then the man in whom the evil spirit

Center column references

8 [b]Acts 1:3; 28:23
*See WW at 2 Thess. 3:4.
9 [a]2 Tim. 1:15; 2 Pet. 2:2; Jude 10 [b]Acts 9:2; 19:23; 22:4; 24:14
10 [a]Acts 19:8; 20:31
11 [a]Mark 16:20; Acts 14:3
12 [a]2 Kin. 4:29; Acts 5:15
13 [a]Matt. 12:27; Luke 11:19 [b]Mark 9:38; Luke 9:49 [c]1 Cor. 1:23; 2:2 1NU / 2adjure, solemnly command

16 1M and they overpowered them 2NU both of them
17 [a]Luke 1:65; 7:16; Acts 2:43; 5:5, 11 *See WW at Acts 5:13.
18 [a]Matt. 3:6
20 [a]Acts 6:7; 12:24 *See WW at 1 Tim. 6:16.
21 [a]Rom. 15:25; Gal. 2:1 [b]Acts 20:22; 2 Cor. 1:16 [c]Acts 20:1; 1 Cor. 16:5 [d]Acts 18:21; 23:11; Rom. 1:13; 15:22–29
22 [a]1 Tim. 1:2 [b]Rom. 16:23; 2 Tim. 4:20
23 [a]2 Cor. 1:8 [b]Acts 9:2
24 [a]Acts 16:16, 19 1Gr. Artemis
26 [a]Deut. 4:28; Ps. 115:4; Is. 44:10–20; Jer. 10:3; Acts 17:29; 1 Cor. 8:4; 10:19; Rev. 9:20 *See WW at Luke 16:4.

was leaped on them, 1overpowered them, and prevailed against 2them, so that they fled out of that house naked and wounded. 17This became known both to all Jews and Greeks dwelling in Ephesus; and [a]fear fell on them all, and the name of the Lord Jesus was *magnified. 18And many who had believed came [a]confessing and telling their deeds. 19Also, many of those who had practiced magic brought their books together and burned *them* in the sight of all. And they counted up the value of them, and *it* totaled fifty thousand *pieces* of silver. 20[a]So the word of the Lord grew *mightily and prevailed.

The Riot at Ephesus

21[a]When these things were accomplished, Paul [b]purposed in the Spirit, when he had passed through [c]Macedonia and Achaia, to go to Jerusalem, saying, "After I have been there, [d]I must also see Rome." 22So he sent into Macedonia two of those who ministered to him, [a]Timothy and [b]Erastus, but he himself stayed in Asia for a time.

23And [a]about that time there arose a great commotion about [b]the Way. 24For a certain man named Demetrius, a silversmith, who made silver shrines of 1Diana, brought [a]no small profit to the craftsmen. 25He called them together with the workers of similar occupation, and said: "Men, you know that we have our prosperity by this trade. 26Moreover you see and hear that not only at Ephesus, but throughout almost all Asia, this Paul has persuaded and *turned away many people, saying that [a]they are

WORD WEALTH

19:20 word, *logos*; Strong's #3056: A transmission of thought, communication, a word of explanation, an utterance, discourse, divine revelation, talk, statement, instruction, an oracle, divine promise, divine doctrine, divine declaration. Jesus is the living *logos* (John 1:1); the Bible is the written *logos* (Heb. 4:12); and the Holy Spirit utters the spoken *logos* (1 Cor. 2:13).

19:8 The kingdom of God: See note on 1:3.

19:12 Handkerchiefs were sweat-rags tied around Paul's head while he was working. See Matt. 9:20, 21 and note on Acts 5:15. Although some find a basis here for using anointed prayer cloths today, the passage does not necessarily provide a warrant for the practice as a formula for ministering divine healing.

19:13–17 The authority of **the name of the Lord Jesus** has been granted only to believers (Mark 16:17; see Luke 10:17–20). The name of Jesus is not given as a magical phrase calculated to guarantee good or bad results. There is no guarantee of power when it is capriciously uttered, particularly when the situation involves an ecclesiastical or stylized exercise. However, when employed in faith by the power of the Holy Spirit, His might and glory may be expected to be manifested. Inherent in the name

of Jesus is not only the resource of His authority, but also the fullness of His nature and character. Thus, any prayer offered or ministry attempted in the name of Jesus must be in accord with His nature and purpose. See note on John 14:13.

19:19 Even in nonbiblical records of the time, Ephesus had the reputation of being a center of magical practices. **Fifty thousand pieces of silver:** This is probably a reference to 50,000 Greek drachmae, a coin which was roughly equivalent to one day's wage, so the cumulative value of these magic books was enormous.

19:24 Diana was the Roman name of Artemis, the Greek goddess of love and fertility; and Ephesus was the home of her great temple (vv. 34, 35), acclaimed as one of the seven wonders of the ancient world.

not gods which are made with hands. 27So not only is this trade of ours in danger of falling into disrepute, but also the temple of the great goddess Diana may be despised and [I]her *magnificence destroyed, whom all Asia and the world worship."

28Now when they heard *this,* they were full of *wrath and cried out, saying, "Great *is* Diana of the Ephesians!" 29So the whole city was filled with confusion, and rushed into the theater with one accord, having seized [a]Gaius and [b]Aristarchus, Macedonians, Paul's travel companions. 30And when Paul wanted to go in to the people, the disciples would not allow him. 31Then some of the [I]officials of Asia, who were his *friends, sent to him pleading that he would not venture into the theater. 32Some therefore cried one thing and some another, for the assembly was confused, and most of them did not know why they had come together. 33And they drew Alexander out of the multitude, the Jews putting him forward. And [a]Alexander [b]motioned with his hand, and wanted to make his defense to the people. 34But when they found out that he was a Jew, all with one voice cried out for about two hours, "Great *is* Diana of the Ephesians!"

35And when the city clerk had quieted the crowd, he said: "Men of Ephesus, what man is there who does not know that the city of the Ephesians is temple guardian of the great goddess [I]Diana, and of the *image* which fell down from [2]Zeus? 36Therefore, since these things cannot be denied, you ought to be quiet and do nothing rashly. 37For you have brought these men here who are neither robbers of temples nor blasphemers of [I]your goddess. 38Therefore, if Demetrius and his fellow craftsmen have a [I]case against anyone, the courts are open and there are proconsuls. Let them bring charges against one another. 39But if you have any other inquiry to make, it shall be determined in the lawful assembly. 40For we are in danger of being [I]called in question for today's uproar, there being no reason which we may *give to account for this disorderly gathering." 41And when he had said these things, he dismissed the assembly.

Journeys in Greece

20 After the uproar had ceased, Paul called the disciples to *himself,* embraced *them,* and [a]departed to go to Mace-

donia. 2Now when he had gone over that region and encouraged them with many words, he came to [a]Greece 3and stayed three months. And [a]when the Jews plotted against him as he was about to sail to Syria, he decided to return through Macedonia. 4And Sopater of Berea accompanied him to Asia—also [a]Aristarchus and Secundus of the Thessalonians, and [b]Gaius of Derbe, and [c]Timothy, and [d]Tychicus and [e]Trophimus of Asia. 5These men, going ahead, waited for us at [a]Troas. 6But we sailed away from Philippi after [a]the Days of Unleavened Bread, and in five days joined them [b]at Troas, where we stayed seven days.

Ministering at Troas

7Now on [a]the first *day* of the week, when the disciples came together [b]to break bread, Paul, ready to depart the next day, spoke to them and continued his message until midnight. 8There were many lamps [a]in the upper room where [I]they were gathered together. 9And in a window sat a certain young man named Eutychus, who was sinking into a deep sleep. He was overcome by sleep; and as Paul continued speaking, he fell down from the third story and was *taken up dead. 10But Paul went down, [a]fell on him, and embracing *him* said, [b]"Do not trouble yourselves, for his life is in him." 11Now when he had come up, had broken bread and *eaten, and talked a long while, even till daybreak, he departed. 12And they brought the young man in alive, and they were not a little comforted.

From Troas to Miletus

13Then we went ahead to the ship and sailed to Assos, there intending to take Paul on board; for so he had [I]given orders, intending himself to go on foot. 14And when he met us at Assos, we took him on board and came to Mitylene. 15We sailed from there, and the next *day* came opposite Chios. The following *day* we arrived at Samos and stayed at Trogyllium. The next *day* we came to Miletus. 16For Paul had decided to sail past Ephesus, so that he would not have to spend time in Asia; for [a]he was hurrying [b]to be at Jerusalem, if *possible, on [c]the Day of Pentecost.

The Ephesian Elders Exhorted

17From Miletus he sent to Ephesus and called for the elders of the *church. 18And

Center cross-reference column

27 [I]NU she be deposed from her magnificence
*See WW at Luke 9:43.
28 *See WW at Luke 4:28.
29 [a]Acts 20:4; Rom. 16:23; 1 Cor. 1:14; 3 John 1 [b]Acts 20:4; 27:2; Col. 4:10; Philem. 24
31 [I]Asiarchs, rulers of Asia, the province
*See WW at John 11:11.
33 [a]1 Tim. 1:20; 2 Tim. 4:14 [b]Acts 12:17
35 [I]Gr. Artemis [2]heaven
37 [I]NU our
38 [I]Lit. matter
40 [I]Or charged with rebellion concerning today
*See WW at Matt. 22:21.

CHAPTER 20
1 [a]1 Cor. 16:5; 1 Tim. 1:3

2 [a]Acts 17:15; 18:1
3 [a]Acts 9:23; 23:12; 25:3; 2 Cor. 11:26
4 [a]Acts 19:29; Col. 4:10 [b]Acts 19:29 [c]Acts 16:1 [d]Eph. 6:21; Col. 4:7; 2 Tim. 4:12; Titus 3:12 [e]Acts 21:29; 2 Tim. 4:20
5 [a]2 Cor. 2:12; 2 Tim. 4:13
6 [a]Ex. 12:14, 15 [b]Acts 16:8; 2 Cor. 2:12; 2 Tim. 4:13
7 [a]1 Cor. 16:2; Rev. 1:10 [b]Acts 2:42, 46; 20:11; 1 Cor. 10:16
8 [a]Acts 1:13 [I]NU, M we
9 *See WW at John 16:22.
10 [a]1 Kin. 17:21; 2 Kin. 4:34 [b]Matt. 9:23, 24; Mark 5:39
11 *See WW at John 8:52.
13 [I]arranged it
16 [a]Acts 18:21; 19:21; 21:4 [b]Acts 24:17 [c]Acts 2:1; 1 Cor. 16:8
*See WW at Matt. 19:26.
17 *See WW at Acts 8:1.

19:32 Another of many references to show that early opposition to Christianity was at times irrational. Anyone who knew the facts would not be threatened by the Christian message (see vv. 36, 37, 40).

20:6 Days of Unleavened Bread was another way to refer to the Passover. See note on Ex. 12:1–11.

20:7 To break bread: See note on 2:42.

20:10 Paul is apparently used by the Holy Spirit in a demonstration of the manifestation of gifts of healings or the working of miracles, in conjunction with the church's continuation of Jesus' ministry. See note on 1:1; 1 Cor. 12:9, 10 and Kingdom Dynamics on Acts 28:8, 9.

WORD WEALTH

20:19 humility, *tapeinophrosunē;* Strong's #5012: Modesty, lowliness, humble-mindedness, a sense of moral insignificance, and a humble attitude of unselfish concern for the welfare of others. It is a total absence of arrogance, conceit, and haughtiness. The word is a combination of *tapeinos,* "humble," and *phrēn,* "mind." The word was unknown in classical nonbiblical Greek. Only by abstaining from self-aggrandizement can members of the Christian community maintain unity and harmony.

when they had come to him, he said to them: "You know, *a*from the first day that I came to Asia, in what manner I always lived among you, [19]serving the Lord with all **humility,** with many tears and trials which happened to me *a*by the plotting of the Jews; [20]how *a*I kept back nothing that was helpful, but proclaimed it to you, and taught you publicly and from house to house, [21a]testifying to Jews, and also to Greeks, *b*repentance toward God and faith toward our Lord Jesus Christ. [22]And see, now *a*I go bound in the spirit to Jerusalem, not knowing the things that will happen to me there, [23]except that *a*the Holy Spirit testifies in every city, saying that chains and tribulations await me. [24][l]But *a*none of these things move me; nor do I count my life dear to myself, *b*so that I may *finish my [2]race with joy, *c*and the ministry *d*which I received from the Lord Jesus, to testify to the gospel of the grace of God.

[25]"And indeed, now I know that you all, among whom I have gone preaching the kingdom of God, will see my face no more. [26]Therefore I testify to you this day that I *am* *a*innocent[l]* of the blood of all *men.*

Cross-references (center column)

18 *a*Acts 18:19; 19:1, 10; 20:4, 16
19 *a*Acts 20:3
20 *a*Acts 20:27
21 *a*Acts 18:5; 19:10 *b*Mark 1:15
22 *a*Acts 19:21
23 *a*Acts 21:4, 11
24 *a*Acts 21:13 *b*Acts 13:25; 2 Tim. 4:7 *c*Acts 1:17 *d*Gal. 1:1 [l]NU But I do not count my life of any value or dear to myself [2]course
*See WW at 1 John 2:5.
26 *a*Acts 18:6; 2 Cor. 7:2 [l]Lit. clean *See WW at Matt. 5:8.
27 *a*Luke 7:30; John 15:15; Eph. 1:11 [l]avoided declaring
28 *a*Luke 12:32; John 21:15–17; Acts 20:29; [1 Tim. 4:16]; 1 Pet. 5:2 *b*1 Cor. 12:28 *c*Eph. 1:7, 14; Col. 1:14; Titus 2:14; Heb. 9:12; [1 Pet. 1:19]; Rev. 5:9 *d*Heb. 9:14 [l]M of the Lord and God
29 *a*Ezek. 22:27; Matt. 7:15
30 *a*1 Tim. 1:20; 2 Tim. 1:15 [l]misleading
31 *a*Acts 19:8, 10; 24:17
32 *a*Heb. 13:9 *b*Acts 9:31 *c*Acts 26:18; Eph. 1:14, 18; 5:5; Col. 1:12; 3:24; [Heb. 9:15; 1 Pet. 1:4] *See WW at John 10:36.
33 *See WW at Matt. 13:17.
34 *a*Acts 18:3;

[27]For I have not [l]shunned to declare to you *a*the whole counsel of God. [28a]Therefore take heed to yourselves and to all the flock, among which the Holy Spirit *b*has made you overseers, to shepherd the church [l]of God *c*which He purchased *d*with His own blood. [29]For I know this, that after my departure *a*savage wolves will come in among you, not sparing the flock. [30]Also *a*from among yourselves men will rise up, speaking [l]perverse things, to draw away the disciples after themselves. [31]Therefore watch, and remember that *a*for three years I did not cease to warn everyone night and day with tears.

[32]"So now, brethren, I commend you to God and *a*to the word of His grace, which is able *b*to build you up and give you *c*an inheritance among all those who are *sanctified. [33]I have *coveted no one's silver or gold or apparel. [34][l]Yes, you yourselves know *a*that these hands have provided for my necessities, and for those who were with me. [35]I have shown you in every way, *a*by laboring like this, that you must support the weak. And remember the words of the Lord Jesus, that He said, 'It is more *blessed to **give** than to receive.' "

WORD WEALTH

20:35 give, *didōmi;* Strong's #1325: Granting, allowing, bestowing, imparting, permitting, placing, offering, presenting, yielding, and paying. *Didōmi* implies giving an object of value. It gives freely and is unforced. Acts 20:35 indicates that the giver takes on the character of Christ, whose nature is to give. Jesus did not say it would be more natural or easier to give than to receive, but that it would be more blessed.

1 Cor. 4:12; 1 Thess. 2:9; 2 Thess. 3:8 [l]NU, M omit *Yes*
35 *a*Rom. 15:1; 1 Cor. 9:12; 2 Cor. 11:9, 12; Eph. 4:28; 1 Thess. 4:11; 2 Thess. 3:8 *See WW at Matt. 5:3.

20:17–35 This was Paul's emotional farewell address to the Ephesian **elders.** In its written form, this passage also became a permanent word of warning and instruction to all the Gentile churches that Paul had established. **Miletus** was a port city that serviced **Ephesus,** about 30 miles away.

20:25 Kingdom of God: Paul does not use this precise phraseology often in his epistles. However, an understanding of its significance (see note on 1:3) shows that it is conceptually synonymous with Paul's more familiar "preaching the gospel, the Cross, or life in the Spirit." See Kingdom Dynamics articles on the kingdom of God.

20:27 The whole counsel of God refers to the larger picture of God's plan. Deception or diminishing of fullness of experience and ministry by the body of Christ often begins when men and women preach only part of the counsel of God.

20:28–32 See section 3 of Truth in Action at the end of Acts.

20:28 This verse is rich with lessons about leadership in the church: (1) **Take heed to yourselves** means "pay close attention." Leaders must first guard themselves before they can oversee the church adequately. (2) Church leaders are not self-made. They are appointed by the Spirit. (3) **Overseers** is from the same Greek

root translated "overshadow" in Luke 1:35. An overseer is one who covers and protects the flock. (4) The church belongs to God. He owns it because He bought it. What God does through the leaders of the church does not belong to them. In contrast, Paul warns of false leaders in Acts 20:29–31.

20:29–31 Characteristics of the wrong kind of leadership in the church: (1) They are more interested in themselves than in the care of the flock (v. 29). (2) They will draw people after themselves (v. 30). (3) They will look for quick results that require little sacrifice (v. 31).

20:32 The word of His grace always builds up and releases our spiritual inheritance. **Are sanctified** is best translated "are being sanctified," with an emphasis on the unfinished process.

20:33–35 This is Paul's view of money and the ministry. Money was not his motivation (v. 33). He supplemented his ministry by making tents (see 18:3), thereby putting less of a financial burden on the churches where he ministered (v. 34). **It is more blessed to give than to receive** refers to our time as well as our money, for **by laboring like this** we **support the weak,** the primary recipients of our giving being those who are less fortunate. This saying of Jesus is not recorded in the Gospels.

36And when he had said these things, he knelt down and prayed with them all. **37**Then they all ᵃwept ¹freely, and ᵇfell on Paul's neck and kissed him, **38**sorrowing most of all for the words which he spoke, that they would *see his face no more. And they accompanied him to the ship.

Warnings on the Journey to Jerusalem

21 Now it came to pass, that when we had departed from them and set sail, running a straight course we came to Cos, the following *day* to Rhodes, and from there to Patara. **2**And finding a ship sailing over to Phoenicia, we went aboard and set sail. **3**When we had sighted Cyprus, we passed it on the left, sailed to Syria, and landed at Tyre; for there the ship was to unload its cargo. **4**And finding ¹disciples,* we stayed there seven days. ᵃThey told Paul through the Spirit not to go up to Jerusalem. **5**When we had come to the end of those days, we departed and went on our way; and they all accompanied us, with wives and children, till *we were* out of the city. And ᵃwe knelt down on the shore and prayed. **6**When we had taken our leave of one another, we boarded the ship, and they returned ᵃhome.

7And when we had finished *our* voyage from Tyre, we came to Ptolemais, greeted the brethren, and stayed with them one day. **8**On the next *day* we ¹who were Paul's companions departed and came to ᵃCaesarea, and entered the house of Philip ᵇthe evangelist, ᶜwho was *one* of the seven, and stayed with him. **9**Now this man had four virgin daughters ᵃwho prophesied. **10**And as we stayed many days, a certain prophet named ᵃAgabus came down from Judea. **11**When he had come to us, he took Paul's belt, bound his *own* hands and feet, and said, "Thus says the Holy Spirit, ᵃ'So shall the Jews at Jerusalem bind the man who owns this belt, and deliver *him* into the hands of the Gentiles.' "

12Now when we heard these things, both we and those from that place pleaded with him not to go up to Jerusalem. **13**Then Paul answered, ᵃ"What do you mean by weeping and breaking my heart? For I am ready not only to be bound, but also to die at Jerusalem for the name of the Lord Jesus." **14**So when he would not be persuaded, we ceased, saying, ᵃ"The *will of the Lord be done."

---

37 ᵃActs 21:13
ᵇGen. 45:14
¹Lit. *much*
38 *See WW at John 20:14.

CHAPTER 21
4 ᵃ[Acts 20:23; 21:12] ¹NU *the disciples*
*See WW at Matt. 10:1.
5 ᵃLuke 22:41; Acts 9:40; 20:36
6 ᵃJohn 1:11
8 ᵃActs 8:40; 21:16 ᵇActs 8:5, 26, 40; Eph. 4:11; 2 Tim. 4:5 ᶜActs 6:5 ¹NU omits *who were Paul's companions*
9 ᵃJoel 2:28; Acts 2:17
10 ᵃActs 11:28
11 ᵃActs 20:23; 21:33; 22:25
13 ᵃActs 20:24, 37
14 ᵃMatt. 6:10; 26:42; Luke 11:2; 22:42 *See WW at Matt. 12:50.

15 ¹made preparations

KINGDOM DYNAMICS

21:9 Women and New Testament Ministry (Philip's Daughters), BIBLICAL WOMEN. This reference to Philip's daughters' each exercising the gifts of prophecy makes clear that women did bring God's word by the power of the Holy Spirit and that such ministry was fully accepted in the early church. This is reinforced by Paul in 1 Corinthians 11:5, where he directs (1) that a woman may "prophesy," but (2) that she must be properly "covered," that is, rightly related to her husband or other spiritual authority, a regulation incumbent upon *all* spiritual leaders—male or female (see 1 Tim. 3:1–13).

It is puzzling why some in the church contest the place of women in ministry. Women had an equal place in the Upper Room, awaiting the Holy Spirit's coming and the birth of the church (Acts 1:14). Then Peter's prophetic sermon at Pentecost affirmed the OT promise was now to be realized: "your daughters" and "maidservants" would now share fully and equally with men in realizing the anointing, fullness, and ministry of the Holy Spirit, making them effective in witness and service for the spread of the gospel.

Though the place of men seems more pronounced in the number who filled leadership offices, there does not appear to be any direct restriction of privilege. Note: (1) The direct mention of Phoebe as a deacon ("servant," Gr. *diakonia*, Rom. 16:1); (2) John's letter to an "elect [chosen] lady" with instructions concerning whom she allows to minister in her "house" (a designation for early church fellowships, 2 John); and (3) 1 Corinthians 1:11 and Philippians 4:2, where Chloe and Euodia seem to be women in whose homes believers gather. The method of designation suggests they were the appointed leaders in their respective fellowships.

The acceptance of women in a public place of ministry in the church is not a concession to the spirit of the feminist movement. But the refusal of such a place might be a concession to an order of male chauvinism, unwarranted by and unsupported in the Scriptures. Clearly, women did speak—preach and prophesy—in the early church (see 1 Tim. 2:8–15). (Acts 9:36/Gen. 4:25*) F.L./J.W.H.

Paul Urged to Make Peace

15And after those days we ¹packed and went up to Jerusalem. **16**Also some of the disciples from Caesarea went with us and brought with them a certain Mnason of Cyprus, an early disciple, with whom we were to lodge.

20:37 Kissed him: See note on Rom. 16:16.

21:4–12 This passage contains several warnings given by the Spirit that Paul would encounter trouble during his visit to Jerusalem (vv. 4, 10–12). But the apostle persisted (v. 14), later being arrested and sent to Rome under guard. Arguments to whether or not Paul was in the perfect will of God are

pointless. What is useful is to note (1) prophecies do not have to dictate the decisions or manipulate the will of a godly person; and 2) even though they may be true, God's purpose may yet be realized, as was the case in God's will ultimately bringing Paul to Rome.

21:10, 11 See note on 11:28.

KINGDOM DYNAMICS

21:11 The Issue of Personal Prophecy, PROPHECY. The Bible clearly allows for personal prophecy. Nathan brought David a confrontive "word" from God (2 Sam. 12:13); Isaiah predicted Hezekiah's death (Is. 38:1); and in this text Agabus told Paul he faced trouble in Jerusalem. "Personal prophecy" refers to a prophecy ("word") the Holy Spirit may prompt one person to give another, relating to personal matters. Many feel deep reservations about this operation of the gift of prophecy because sometimes it is abused. True "words" may be used to manipulate others, or they may be unwisely or hastily applied. This passage reveals safeguards against abusive uses of personal prophecy, allowing us to implement this biblical practice. *First*, the "word" will usually not be new to the mind of the person addressed, but it will confirm something God is already dealing with him about. From Acts 20:22–24 we know Paul was already sensitive to the issue Agabus raised. *Second*, the character of the person bringing the "word" ought to be weighed. Agabus's credibility is related not to his claim of having a "word," but to his record as a trustworthy man of God used in the exercise of this gift (11:28; 21:10). *Third*, remember that the prophecy, or "word," is not to be considered "controlling." In other words,

17ᵃAnd when we had come to Jerusalem, the brethren received us gladly. 18On the following *day* Paul went in with us to ᵃJames, and all the elders were present. 19When he had greeted them, ᵃhe told in detail those things which God had done among the Gentiles ᵇthrough his ministry. 20And when they heard *it*, they glorified the Lord. And they said to him, "You see, brother, how many myriads of Jews there are who have believed, and they are all ᵃzealous* for the law; 21but they have been informed about you that you teach all the Jews who are among the Gentiles to *forsake Moses, saying that they ought not to circumcise *their* children nor to walk according to the customs. 22ᶦWhat then? The assembly must certainly meet, for they will hear that you have come. 23Therefore do what we tell you: We have four men who have taken a vow. 24Take them and be purified with them, and pay their expenses so that they may ᵃshave *their* heads, and that all may know that

Cross-references (center column):
17 ᵃActs 15:4
18 ᵃActs 15:13; Gal. 1:19; 2:9
19 ᵃActs 15:4, 12; Rom. 15:18, 19
ᵇActs 1:17; 20:24; 1 Tim. 2:7
20 ᵃActs 15:1; 22:3; [Rom. 10:2]; Gal. 1:14
*See WW at Acts 22:3.
21 *See WW at 2 Thess. 2:3.
22 ᶦNU *What then is to be done? They will certainly hear*
24 ᵃNum. 6:2, 13, 18; Acts 18:18

25 ᵃActs 15:19, 20, 29 ᶦNU omits *that they should observe no such thing, except* ²*fornication*
*See WW at Matt. 15:19.
26 ᵃJohn 11:55; Acts 21:24; 24:18
ᵇNum. 6:13; Acts 24:18
ᶦ*completion*
*See WW at Heb. 9:28.

such prophecies should never be perceived as dominating anyone's free will. Christian living is never cultish—governed by omens or the counsel of gurus. Paul did not change his plans because of Agabus's prophecy or because of the urging of others (vv. 12–14); he received the "word" graciously but continued his plans nonetheless. *Fourth*, all prophecy is "in part" (1 Cor. 13:9), which means that as true as that "part" may be, it does not give the whole picture. Agabus's "word" was true, and Paul was bound in Jerusalem. But this also occasioned an opportunity to eventually minister in Rome (Acts 23:11). *Finally*, in the light of a "word," we should prayerfully consider the word as Mary did the shepherds' report (Luke 2:19). A hasty response is never required: simply wait on God. We should then move ahead with trust in God, as Hezekiah did. He had been told that he would shortly die; but he prayed instead of merely surrendering to the prophecy, and his life realized its intended length—unshortened by his diseased condition. Occasional personal prophecy is not risky if kept on biblical footings, but neither is it to become the way we plan or direct our lives. (2 Pet. 1:16–19/Acts 11:27–30) J.W.H.

WORD WEALTH

21:26 offering, *prosphora;* Strong's #4376: A bringing to, setting before, presenting, sacrificing, a gift, the act of offering, or the thing offered. The word includes giving kindness and bestowing benefit. Paul engaged in the purification ceremony. It was not necessary for his salvation, but was an act of devotion to God. Paul's principle was being all things to all men in order to win them.

those things of which they were informed concerning you are nothing, but *that* you yourself also walk orderly and keep the law. 25But concerning the Gentiles who believe, ᵃwe have written *and* decided ᶦthat they should observe no such thing, except that they should keep themselves from *things* offered to idols, from blood, from things strangled, and from ²sexual* immorality."

Arrested in the Temple

26Then Paul took the men, and the next day, having been purified with them, ᵃentered the temple ᵇto announce the ᶦexpiration of the days of purification, at which time an **offering** should be *made for each one of them.

21:18 James: See note on 12:17.

21:20–25 There was still wide debate about Paul's teaching and Gentile Christianity (v. 21). So the apostolic leadership in Jerusalem asked Paul, out of courtesy to those who were suspicious of him, to purify himself ceremonially. The apostles themselves, however, knew that the accusations were baseless (v. 24). Furthermore, the decree of the Jerusalem Council

(ch. 15) was **written and decided** (v. 25).

21:24 Pay their expenses was a pious and charitable way for an Israelite to associate himself with those who had taken a Nazirite vow (see note on Num. 6:1–21). This involved 30 days of ritual purification, including shaving the head.

21:25 This is a reaffirmation of the apostolic decree in 15:19, 20.

27Now when the seven days were almost ended, ᵃthe Jews from Asia, seeing him in the temple, stirred up the whole crowd and ᵇlaid hands on him, 28crying out, "Men of Israel, help! This is the man ᵃwho teaches all men everywhere against the people, the law, and this place; and furthermore he also brought Greeks into the temple and has defiled this holy place." 29(For they had ˡpreviously seen ᵃTrophimus the Ephesian with him in the city, whom they supposed that Paul had brought into the temple.)

30And ᵃall the city was disturbed; and the people ran together, seized Paul, and dragged him out of the temple; and *immediately the doors were shut. 31Now as they were ᵃseeking to kill him, news came to the commander of the ˡgarrison that all Jerusalem was in an uproar. 32ᵃHe immediately took soldiers and centurions, and ran down to them. And when they saw the commander and the soldiers, they stopped beating Paul. 33Then the ᵃcommander came near and took him, and ᵇcommanded him to be bound with two chains; and he asked who he was and what he had done. 34And some among the multitude cried one thing and some another.

So when he could not ascertain the truth because of the tumult, he commanded him to be taken into the barracks. 35When he reached the stairs, he had to be carried by the soldiers because of the violence of the mob. 36For the multitude of the people followed after, crying out, ᵃ"Away with him!"

Addressing the Jerusalem Mob

37Then as Paul was about to be led into the barracks, he said to the commander, "May I speak to you?"

He replied, "Can you speak Greek? 38ᵃAre you not the Egyptian who some time ago stirred up a rebellion and led the four thousand assassins out into the wilderness?"

39But Paul said, ᵃ"I am a Jew from Tarsus, in Cilicia, a citizen of no ˡmean city; and I implore you, permit me to speak to the people."

40So when he had given him permission,

Paul stood on the stairs and ᵃmotioned with his hand to the people. And when there was a great silence, he spoke to *them in the ᵇHebrew language, saying,

22 "Brethrenᵃ and fathers, hear my defense before you now." 2And when they heard that he spoke to them in the ᵃHebrew language, they kept all the more silent.

Then he said: 3ᵃ"I am indeed a Jew, born in Tarsus of Cilicia, but brought up in this city ᵇat the feet of ᶜGamaliel, taught ᵈaccording to the strictness of our fathers' law, and ᵉwas zealous toward God ᶠas you all are today. 4ᵃI persecuted this Way to the death, binding and delivering into prisons both men and women, 5as also the high priest bears me witness, and ᵃall the council of the *elders, ᵇfrom whom I also received letters to the brethren, and went to Damascus ᶜto bring in chains even those who were there to Jerusalem to be punished.

6"Now ᵃit happened, as I journeyed and came near Damascus at about noon, suddenly a great light from heaven shone around me. 7And I fell to the ground and heard a voice saying to me, 'Saul, Saul, why are you persecuting Me?' 8So I answered, 'Who are You, Lord?' And He said to me, 'I am Jesus of Nazareth, whom you are persecuting.'

9"And ᵃthose who were with me indeed saw the light ˡand were afraid, but they did not hear the voice of Him who spoke to me. 10So I said, 'What shall I do, Lord?' And the Lord said to me, 'Arise and go into Damascus, and there you will be told all things which are appointed for you to do.' 11And

Cross-references (center column):

27 ᵃActs 20:19; 24:18 ᵇActs 26:21
28 ᵃ[Matt. 24:15]; Acts 6:13; 24:6
29 ᵃActs 20:4 ˡM omits previously
30 ᵃ2 Kin. 11:15; Acts 16:19; 26:21 *See WW at John 6:21.
31 ᵃ2 Cor. 11:23 ˡcohort
32 ᵃActs 23:27; 24:7
33 ᵃActs 24:7 ᵇActs 20:23; 21:11; Eph. 6:20; 2 Tim. 1:16; 2:9
36 ᵃLuke 23:18; John 19:15; Acts 22:22
38 ᵃActs 5:36
39 ᵃActs 9:11; 22:3; 2 Cor. 11:22; Phil. 3:4–6 ˡinsignificant

40 ᵃActs 12:17 ᵇJohn 5:2; Acts 22:2

CHAPTER 22
1 ᵃActs 7:2
2 ᵃActs 21:40
3 ᵃActs 21:39; 2 Cor. 11:22 ᵇDeut. 33:3 ᶜActs 5:34 ᵈActs 23:6; 26:5; Phil. 3:6 ᵉActs 21:20; Gal. 1:14 ᶠ[Rom. 10:2]
4 ᵃActs 8:3; 26:9–11; Phil. 3:6; 1 Tim. 1:13
5 ᵃActs 23:14; 24:1; 25:15 ᵇLuke 22:66; Acts 4:5; 1 Tim. 4:14 ᶜActs 9:2 *See WW at 1 Tim. 4:14.
6 ᵃActs 9:3; 26:12, 13
9 ᵃDan. 10:7; Acts 9:7 ˡNU omits and were afraid

WORD WEALTH

22:3 zealous, *zēlōtēs;* Strong's #2207: Burning with zeal, having warmth and feeling for or against, deep commitment and eager devotion to something or someone, an enthusiast, uncompromising partisan, admirer, emulator, imitator, follower of anyone. Paul rejected his previous zeal that caused him to become a persecutor of the church, but rejoiced in his *zēlōtēs* for the Lord Jesus Christ.

21:27–29 The ploy of vv. 23, 24 does not work. These Asian Jews, who made the pilgrimage to Jerusalem for the feast, had opposed Paul in their regions. When some of them recognized Paul himself in the temple, they were enraged, especially when they mistakenly thought he had brought Trophimus, a Gentile, with him into the inner temple precincts. This was an offense so grave that even Roman citizens were not exempt from its death penalty.

21:30–32 The prophecy of Agabus and the warnings of the church are fulfilled (see 21:4, 11, 12).

22:2 The Hebrew language is probably a reference to Aramaic, a dialect related to Hebrew.

22:3 Gamaliel: See note on 5:33–40.

22:6 This begins the second of three Pauline conversion narratives in Acts. The first (9:1–19) was Luke's account of the event. The second (vv. 6–21) and the third (26:12–18) were told by Paul himself in his public testimony to the Jews and later to the authorities.

22:7, 8 See note on 9:4.

22:9 Did not hear the voice seems to contradict 9:7, where Luke records that they did hear the voice. Actually, the verses contain different grammatical constructions, which say the same thing. The companions of Paul heard the sound of the voice, but did not discern words with understanding.

since I could not see for the glory of that light, being led by the hand of those who were with me, I came into Damascus.

12"Then ^aa certain Ananias, a devout man according to the law, ^bhaving a good testimony with all the ^cJews who dwelt *there*, 13came to me; and he stood and said to me, 'Brother Saul, receive your sight.' And at that same hour I looked up at him. 14Then he said, ^a"The God of our fathers ^bhas chosen you that you should ^cknow His will, and ^dsee the Just One, ^eand hear the voice of His mouth. 15^aFor you will be His witness to all men of ^bwhat you have seen and heard. 16And now why are you waiting? Arise and be baptized, ^aand wash away your sins, ^bcalling on the name of the Lord.'

17"Now ^ait happened, when I returned to Jerusalem and was praying in the temple, that I was in a trance 18and ^asaw Him saying to me, ^b'Make haste and get out of Jerusalem quickly, for they will not receive your *testimony concerning Me.' 19So I said, 'Lord, ^athey know that in every synagogue I imprisoned and ^bbeat those who believe on You. 20^aAnd when the blood of Your martyr Stephen was shed, I also was standing by ^bconsenting ^lto his death, and guarding the clothes of those who were killing him.' 21Then He said to me, 'Depart, ^afor I will send you far from here to the Gentiles.' "

Paul's Roman Citizenship

22And they listened to him until this word, and *then* they raised their voices and said, ^a"Away with such a *fellow* from the earth, for ^bhe is not fit to live!" 23Then, as they cried out and ^ltore off *their* clothes and threw dust into the air, 24the commander ordered him to be brought into the barracks, and said that he should be examined under scourging, so that he might know why they shouted so against him. 25And as they bound him with thongs, Paul said to the centurion who stood by, ^a"Is it lawful for you to scourge a man who is a Roman, and uncondemned?"

26When the centurion heard *that,* he went and told the commander, saying, "Take care what you do, for this man is a Roman."

27Then the commander came and said to him, "Tell me, are you a Roman?"

He said, "Yes."

28The commander answered, "With a large sum I obtained this citizenship."

And Paul said, "But I was born a *citizen.*"

29Then immediately those who were about to examine him withdrew from him; and the commander was also afraid after he found out that he was a Roman, and because he had bound him.

The Sanhedrin Divided

30The next day, because he wanted to know for certain why he was accused by the Jews, he released him from *his* bonds, and commanded the chief priests and all their council to appear, and brought Paul down and set him before them.

23 Then Paul, looking earnestly at the council, said, "Men *and* brethren, ^aI have lived in all good conscience before God until this day." 2And the high priest Ananias commanded those who stood by him ^ato strike him on the mouth. 3Then Paul said to him, "God will strike you, *you* whitewashed wall! For you sit to judge me according to the law, and ^ado you command me to be struck contrary to the law?"

4And those who stood by said, "Do you revile God's high priest?"

5Then Paul said, ^a"I did not know, brethren, that he was the high priest; for it is written, ^b'You shall not speak evil of a ruler of your people.' "

6But when Paul perceived that one part were Sadducees and the other Pharisees, he cried out in the council, "Men *and* brethren, ^aI am a Pharisee, the son of a Pharisee; ^bconcerning the hope and resurrection of the dead I am being judged!"

7And when he had said this, a dissension arose between the Pharisees and

Cross references (center column)

12 ^aActs 9:17
^bActs 10:22
^c1 Tim. 3:7
14 ^aActs 3:13;
5:30 ^bActs
9:15; 26:16;
Gal. 1:15
^cActs 3:14;
7:52 ^dActs
9:17; 26:16;
1 Cor. 9:1; 15:8
^e1 Cor. 11:23;
Gal. 1:12
15 ^aActs 23:11
^bActs 4:20;
26:16
16 ^aActs 2:38;
1 Cor. 6:11;
[Eph. 5:26];
Heb. 10:22
^bActs 9:14;
Rom. 10:13
17 ^aActs 9:26;
26:20; 2 Cor.
12:2
18 ^aActs 22:14
^bMatt. 10:14
*See WW at
John 19:35.
19 ^aActs 8:3;
22:4 ^bMatt.
10:17; Acts
26:11
20 ^aActs
7:54—8:1
^bLuke 11:48
^lNU omits *to
his death*
21 ^aActs 9:15;
Rom. 1:5;
11:13; Gal. 2:7,
8; Eph. 3:7,
8; 1 Tim. 2:7;
2 Tim. 1:11
22 ^aActs 21:36;
1 Thess. 2:16
^bActs 25:24
23 ^lLit. threw
25 ^aActs 16:37

CHAPTER 23
1 ^aActs 24:16;
1 Cor. 4:4;
2 Cor. 1:12;
4:2; 2 Tim. 1:3;
Heb. 13:18
2 ^a1 Kin. 22:24;
Jer. 20:2; John
18:22
3 ^aLev. 19:35;
Deut. 25:1, 2;
John 7:51
5 ^aLev. 5:17, 18
^bEx. 22:28;
Eccl. 10:20;
2 Pet. 2:10
6 ^aActs 26:5;
Phil. 3:5 ^bActs
24:15, 21;
26:6; 28:20

Footnotes (bottom)

22:12 The description of **Ananias** here is to show how Paul's conversion and subsequent ministry were compatible with Jewish traditions.

22:16 See note on **be baptized,** 2:38.

22:18 They will not receive your testimony refers to the general Jewish leadership and community in Jerusalem, not to the church (see 9:26–28).

22:22 Mention of the "Gentiles" (v. 21) infuriated the Jews.

22:23 Luke is reporting the utter madness of the opposition to Paul and the Christian message he represented (see 23:10). Throughout Acts, believers are shown to be rational; their detractors, irrational (26:24–26). The message of Jesus and the Cross is foolishness to the world, but to those who are saved, it is utterly reasonable. The gospel is the wisdom and power of God (1 Cor. 1:18–25).

22:24 The response of the crowd was so outrageous that the Roman authorities suspected Paul of some greater crime, for which they would force a confession by scourging.

22:25 For his own protection, Paul appeals to his Roman citizenship (see note on 16:37).

23:2 Ananias, the high priest, is different from the Ananias of 5:1 and 9:10.

23:3–5 Whitewashed wall means new and clean appearance, but rotten on the inside. Perhaps Paul's reaction was improper (see v. 5; 1 Pet. 2:21–23), but even Jesus defended His legal rights (John 18:21–23). **I did not know . . . he was the high priest** may have been spoken in bitter irony, indicating he did not expect to receive justice from the Jewish court.

23:6 See notes on Matt. 16:6; 22:31, 32.

WORD ⚔ WEALTH

23:6 resurrection, *anastasis*; Strong's #386: A standing up again, restoration to life, rising from the dead. A compound of *ana*, "again," and *histēmi*, "to stand." The resurrection of Jesus is the firstfruits or prototype of the future resurrection of all that are in the grave. In verse 6, *anastasis* is the coming resurrection that occurs at the Judgment Day. Another usage of *anastasis* is "a moral recovery of spiritual truth."

WORD ⚔ WEALTH

23:11 be of good cheer, *tharseō*; Strong's #2293: Derived from a word meaning "courage," this Greek verb is used only eight times in the NT, and seven of the eight are spoken by Jesus. Twice He uses it to refute His disciples' fear (Matt. 14:27; Mark 6:50); on other occasions He uses it to comfort the sick prior to miraculous healing (Matt. 9:2) or just afterward (Luke 8:48). In John 16:33, the imperative is more general: "In the world you will have tribulation; but be of good cheer, I have overcome the world." The word is also used in Matthew 9:22 and Mark 10:49.

the Sadducees; and the assembly was divided. 8 ᵃFor Sadducees say that there is no resurrection—and no angel or spirit; but the Pharisees confess both. 9Then there arose a loud outcry. And the scribes of the Pharisees' party arose and protested, saying, ᵃ"We find no evil in this man; ᶦbut ᵇif a spirit or an angel has spoken to him, ᶜlet us not fight against God."

10Now when there arose a great dissension, the commander, fearing lest Paul might be pulled to pieces by them, commanded the soldiers to go down and *take him by force from among them, and bring *him* into the barracks.

The Plot Against Paul

11But ᵃthe following night the Lord stood by him and said, ᶦ"**Be of good cheer**, Paul; for as you have testified for Me in ᵇJerusalem, so you must also bear witness at ᶜRome."

12And when it was day, ᵃsome of the Jews banded together and bound themselves under an oath, saying that they would neither eat nor drink till they had ᵇkilled Paul. 13Now there were more than forty who had

Marginal references

8 ᵃMatt. 22:23; Mark 12:18; Luke 20:27
9 ᵃActs 25:25; 26:31 ᵇJohn 12:29; Acts 22:6, 7, 17, 18 ᶜActs 5:39 ᶦNU *what if a spirit or an angel has spoken to him?* omitting the last clause
10 *See WW at 1 Thess. 4:17.
11 ᵃActs 18:9; 27:23, 24 ᵇActs 21:18, 19; 22:1–21 ᶜActs 28:16, 17, 23 ᶦTake courage
12 ᵃActs 23:21, 30; 25:3 ᵇActs 9:23, 24; 25:3; 26:21; 27:42; 1 Thess. 2:15

14 ᵃActs 4:5, 23; 6:12; 22:5; 24:1; 25:15
*See WW at 1 Cor. 12:3.
15 ᶦNU omits *tomorrow*
*See WW at John 14:21.
20 ᵃActs 23:12
22 *See WW at John 14:21.
23 ᵃActs 8:40; 23:33
*See WW at Rev. 21:2.
27 ᵃActs 21:30, 33; 24:7

formed this conspiracy. 14They came to the chief priests and ᵃelders, and said, "We have bound ourselves under a great *oath that we will eat nothing until we have killed Paul. 15Now you, therefore, together with the council, *suggest to the commander that he be brought down to you ᶦtomorrow, as though you were going to make further inquiries concerning him; but we are ready to kill him before he comes near."

16So when Paul's sister's son heard of their ambush, he went and entered the barracks and told Paul. 17Then Paul called one of the centurions to *him* and said, "Take this young man to the commander, for he has something to tell him." 18So he took him and brought *him* to the commander and said, "Paul the prisoner called me to *him* and asked *me* to bring this young man to you. He has something to say to you."

19Then the commander took him by the hand, went aside, and asked privately, "What is it that you have to tell me?"

20And he said, ᵃ"The Jews have agreed to ask that you bring Paul down to the council tomorrow, as though they were going to inquire more fully about him. 21But do not yield to them, for more than forty of them lie in wait for him, men who have bound themselves by an oath that they will neither eat nor drink till they have killed him; and now they are ready, waiting for the promise from you."

22So the commander let the young man depart, and commanded *him*, "Tell no one that you have *revealed these things to me."

Sent to Felix

23And he called for two centurions, saying, *"Prepare two hundred soldiers, seventy horsemen, and two hundred spearmen to go to ᵃCaesarea at the third hour of the night; 24and provide mounts to set Paul on, and bring *him* safely to Felix the governor." 25He wrote a letter in the following manner:

26 Claudius Lysias,

To the most excellent governor Felix:

Greetings.

27 ᵃThis man was seized by the Jews and was about to be killed by them. Coming with the troops I rescued him, having learned that he was a

---

23:11 See note on 21:4–12.
23:16 God speaks through angels, dreams, and visions. At other times He uses people and very ordinary situations. What at first may appear to be everyday circumstances are actually God's providences.

23:24 Felix served as **governor** of Judea from A.D. 52 to 59 (see note on 25:13).

Roman. 28ᵃAnd when I wanted to know the reason they accused him, I brought him before their council. 29I found out that he was accused ᵃconcerning questions of their law, ᵇbut had nothing charged against him deserving of death or chains. 30And ᵃwhen it was told me that ᴵthe Jews lay in wait for the man, I sent him immediately to you, and ᵇalso commanded his accusers to state before you the charges against him.

Farewell.

31Then the soldiers, as they were commanded, took Paul and brought *him* by night to Antipatris. 32The next day they left the horsemen to go on with him, and returned to the barracks. 33When they came to ᵃCaesarea and had delivered the ᵇletter to the governor, they also presented Paul to him. 34And when the governor had read *it*, he asked what province he was from. And when he understood that *he was* from ᵃCilicia, 35he said, ᵃ"I will hear you when your accusers also have come." And he commanded him to be kept in ᵇHerod's ᴵPraetorium.

Accused of Sedition

24 Now after ᵃfive days ᵇAnanias the high priest came down with the elders and a certain orator *named* Tertullus. These *gave evidence to the governor against Paul.

2And when he was called upon, Tertullus began his accusation, saying: "Seeing that through you we enjoy great peace, and ᴵprosperity is being brought to this nation by your *foresight, 3we accept *it* always and in all places, most noble Felix, with all thankfulness. 4Nevertheless, not to be

WORD **WEALTH**

24:4 courtesy, *epieikeia;* Strong's #1932: Graciousness, gentleness, clemency, moderation, sweet reasonableness, mildness, fairness, kindness, forbearance, what is right or fitting. In 2 Corinthians 10:1, *epieikeia* is an attribute of God. Here it is an appeal to Felix to show the customary graciousness befitting his high office. Christians can display *epieikeia* in virtue of their divine calling.

28 ᵃActs 22:30
29 ᵃActs 18:15; 25:19 ᵇActs 25:25; 26:31
30 ᵃActs 23:20 ᵇActs 24:8; 25:6 ᴵNU there would be a plot against the man
33 ᵃActs 8:40 ᵇActs 23:26–30
34 ᵃActs 6:9; 21:39
35 ᵃActs 24:1, 10; 25:16 ᵇMatt. 27:27 ᴵHeadquarters

CHAPTER 24
1 ᵃActs 21:27 ᵇActs 23:2, 30, 35; 25:2 *See WW at John 14:21.
2 ᴵOr reforms are *See WW at Rom. 13:14.
4 ᴵgraciousness
5 ᵃLuke 23:2; Acts 6:13; 16:20; 17:6; 21:28; 1 Pet. 2:12, 15 *See WW at 2 Pet. 2:1.
6 ᵃActs 21:28 ᵇJohn 18:31 ᴵNU ends the sentence here and omits the rest of v. 6, all of v. 7, and the first clause of v. 8.
7 ᵃActs 21:33; 23:10
8 ᵃActs 23:30
9 ᴵNU, M joined the attack
11 ᵃActs 21:15, 18, 26, 27; 24:17 *See WW at Rev. 4:10.
12 ᵃActs 25:8; 28:17
14 ᵃAmos 8:14; Acts 9:2; 24:22 ᵇ2 Tim. 1:3 ᶜActs 26:22; 28:23 *See WW at 2 Pet. 2:1.
15 ᵃActs 23:6; 26:6, 7; 28:20 ᵇDan. 12:2; John 5:28, 29; 11:24] ᴵNU omits of the dead *See WW at Acts 23:6.
16 ᵃActs 23:1
17 ᵃActs 11:29, 30; Rom. 15:25–28; 1 Cor. 16:1–4; 2 Cor. 8:1–4; 9:1, 2, 12; Gal. 2:10 *See WW at Acts 21:26.
18 ᵃActs 21:27; 26:21 ᵇActs 21:26

tedious to you any further, I beg you to hear, by your ᴵcourtesy, a few words from us. 5ᵃFor we have found this man a plague, a creator of dissension among all the Jews throughout the world, and a ringleader of the *sect of the Nazarenes. 6ᵃHe even tried to profane the temple, and we seized him, ᴵand wanted ᵇto judge him according to our law. 7ᵃBut the commander Lysias came by and with great violence took *him* out of our hands, 8ᵃcommanding his accusers to come to you. By examining him yourself you may ascertain all these things of which we accuse him." 9And the Jews also ᴵassented, maintaining that these things were so.

The Defense Before Felix

10Then Paul, after the governor had nodded to him to speak, answered: "Inasmuch as I know that you have been for many years a judge of this nation, I do the more cheerfully answer for myself, 11because you may ascertain that it is no more than twelve days since I went up to Jerusalem ᵃto *worship. 12ᵃAnd they neither found me in the temple disputing with anyone nor inciting the crowd, either in the synagogues or in the city. 13Nor can they prove the things of which they now accuse me. 14But this I confess to you, that according to ᵃthe Way which they call a *sect, so I worship the ᵇGod of my fathers, believing all things which are written in ᶜthe Law and in the Prophets. 15ᵃI have hope in God, which they themselves also accept, ᵇthat there will be a *resurrection ᴵof *the* dead, both of *the* just and *the* unjust. 16ᵃThis *being* so, I myself always strive to have a conscience without offense toward God and men.

17"Now after many years ᵃI came to bring alms and *offerings to my nation, 18ᵃin the midst of which some Jews from Asia found me ᵇpurified in the temple, neither with a mob nor with tumult. 19ᵃThey ought to have been here before you to object if they had anything against me. 20Or else let those who are *here* themselves say ᴵif they found any wrongdoing in me while I stood before the council, 21unless *it is* for this one statement which I cried out, standing among them, ᵃ'Concerning the resurrection of the dead I am being judged by you this day.'"

19 ᵃ[Acts 23:30; 25:16] 20 ᴵNU, M what wrongdoing they found 21 ᵃ[Acts 23:6; 24:15; 28:20]

24:2, 3 A proper but manipulative introduction. In contrast, Paul's introduction is polite, but direct.

24:5 The sect of the Nazarenes, a moderately derisive name given to the Christians (see v. 14, "which they call a sect").

24:10 See note on vv. 2, 3.

24:14 Believing all things which are written in the Law and

in the Prophets: The followers of Jesus did not reject the Jewish Scriptures (see Matt. 5:17, 18). They simply understood them in a new light: Jesus of Nazareth was the Messiah (Acts 18:5); His Coming was not merely to fulfill Jewish national interests (1:6, 7); and His kingdom included all nations—the Gentiles (15:15–17). See 26:6, 7, 22, 23; note on 28:23.

24:18 See note on 21:23, 24.

Felix Procrastinates

22But when Felix heard these things, having more accurate knowledge of the aWay, he adjourned the proceedings and said, "When bLysias the commander comes down, I will make a decision on your case." 23So he commanded the centurion to keep Paul and to let *him* have liberty, and atold him not to forbid any of his friends to provide for or visit him.

24And after some days, when Felix came with his wife Drusilla, who was Jewish, he sent for Paul and heard him concerning the afaith in Christ. 25Now as he reasoned about *righteousness, self-control, and the *judgment to come, Felix was afraid and answered, "Go away for now; when I have a convenient time I will call for you." 26Meanwhile he also hoped that amoney would be given him by Paul, lthat he might release him. Therefore he sent for him more often and conversed with him.

27But after two years Porcius Festus succeeded Felix; and Felix, awanting* to do the Jews a favor, left Paul bound.

Paul Appeals to Caesar

25 Now when Festus had come to the province, after three days he went up from aCaesarea to Jerusalem. 2aThen the lhigh priest and the chief men of the Jews *informed him against Paul; and they petitioned him, 3asking a favor against him, that he would summon him to Jerusalem—awhile *they* lay in ambush along the road to kill him. 4But Festus answered that Paul should be kept at Caesarea, and that he himself was going *there* shortly. 5"Therefore," he said, "let those who have authority among you go down with *me* and accuse this man, to see aif there is any fault in him."

6And when he had remained among them more than ten days, he went down to Caesarea. And the next day, sitting on the *judgment seat, he commanded Paul to be brought. 7When he had come, the Jews who had come down from Jerusalem stood about aand laid many serious complaints against Paul, which they could not prove, 8while he answered for himself, a"Neither against the law of the Jews, nor against the temple, nor against Caesar have I offended in anything at all."

WORD WEALTH

25:10 I have done no wrong, *adikeō;* Strong's #91: To do an injustice, to act criminally or unrighteously, to violate any human or divine law, to do wrong, to mistreat others. The word is a compound of *a,* "without," and *dike,* "right"; hence, an illegal action. *Adikeō* consists of offending legally, general wrongdoing, social injustice, and inflicting hurt or damage on individuals. In his appeal to Caesar, Paul declares his innocence.

9But Festus, awanting to do the Jews a favor, answered Paul and said, b"Are you *willing to go up to Jerusalem and there be judged before me concerning these things?"

10So Paul said, "I stand at Caesar's judgment seat, where I ought to be judged. To the Jews **I have done no wrong,** as you very well know. 11aFor if I am an offender, or have committed anything deserving of death, I do not object to dying; but if there is nothing in these things of which these men accuse me, no one can deliver me to them. bI appeal to Caesar."

12Then Festus, when he had conferred with the council, answered, "You have appealed to Caesar? To Caesar you shall go!"

Paul Before Agrippa

13And after some days King Agrippa and Bernice came to Caesarea to greet Festus. 14When they had been there many days, Festus laid Paul's case before the king, saying: a"There is a certain man left a prisoner by Felix, 15aabout whom the chief priests and the elders of the Jews *informed *me,* when I was in Jerusalem, asking for a judgment against him. 16aTo them I answered, 'It is not the custom of the Romans to deliver any man lto destruction before the accused meets the accusers face to face, and has opportunity to answer for himself concerning the charge against him.' 17Therefore when they had come together, awithout any delay, the next day I sat on the judgment seat and commanded the man to be brought in. 18When the accusers stood up, they brought no accusation against him of such things as I lsupposed, 19abut had some questions against him about their own religion and about a certain Jesus, who had died, whom Paul affirmed to be alive. 20And because I was uncertain of such questions, I asked whether he was willing to go to Jerusalem and there be judged concerning these matters. 21But when Paul ªappealed to be reserved for the decision of Augustus, I commanded him to be kept till I could send him to Caesar."

22Then ªAgrippa said to Festus, "I also would like to hear the man myself."

"Tomorrow," he said, "you shall hear him."

23So the next day, when Agrippa and Bernice had come with great ¹pomp, and had entered the auditorium with the commanders and the prominent men of the city, at Festus' command ªPaul was brought in. 24And Festus said: "King Agrippa and all the men who are here present with us, you see this man about whom ªthe whole assembly of the Jews *petitioned me, both at Jerusalem and here, crying out that he was ᵇnot fit to live any longer. 25But when I *found that ªhe had committed nothing deserving of death, ᵇand that he himself had appealed to Augustus, I decided to send him. 26I have nothing certain to write to my lord concerning him. Therefore I have brought him out before you, and especially before you, King Agrippa, so that after the examination has taken place I may have something to write. 27For it seems to me unreasonable to send a prisoner and not to specify the charges against him."

Paul's Early Life

26 Then Agrippa said to Paul, "You are permitted to speak for yourself."

So Paul stretched out his hand and answered for himself: 2"I think myself ªhappy, King Agrippa, because today I shall answer ᵇfor myself before you concerning all the things of which I am ᶜaccused by the Jews, 3especially because you are expert in all customs and questions which have to do with the Jews. Therefore I beg you to hear me patiently.

4"My manner of life from my youth, which was spent from the beginning among my own nation at Jerusalem, all the Jews know. 5They knew me from the first, if they were willing to testify, that according to ªthe strictest *sect of our religion I lived a Pharisee. 6ªAnd now I stand and am *judged for the hope of ᵇthe promise made by God to our fathers. 7To this *promise* ªour twelve tribes, earnestly serving God ᵇnight and day,

ᶜhope to attain. For this hope's sake, King Agrippa, I am accused by the Jews. 8Why should it be thought incredible by you that God raises the dead?

9ª"Indeed, I myself thought I must do many things ¹contrary to the name of ᵇJesus of Nazareth. 10ªThis I also did in Jerusalem, and many of the saints I shut up in prison, having received authority ᵇfrom the chief priests; and when they were put to death, I cast my vote against *them*. 11ªAnd I punished them often in every synagogue and compelled *them* to blaspheme; and being exceedingly enraged against them, I persecuted *them* even to foreign cities.

Paul Recounts His Conversion

12ª"While thus occupied, as I journeyed to Damascus with authority and commission from the chief priests, 13at midday, O king, along the road I saw a light from heaven, brighter than the sun, shining around me and those who journeyed with me. 14And when we all had fallen to the ground, I heard a voice speaking to me and saying in the Hebrew language, 'Saul, Saul, why are you persecuting Me? *It is* hard for you to kick against the goads.' 15So I said, 'Who are You, Lord?' And He said, 'I am Jesus, whom you are persecuting. 16But rise and stand on your feet; for I have appeared to you for this purpose, ªto make you a minister and a *witness both of the things which you have seen and of the things which I will yet reveal to you. 17I will ¹deliver you from the Jewish people, as well as *from* the Gentiles, ªto whom I ²now send you, 18ªto open their eyes, *in order* ᵇto turn *them* from darkness to light, and *from* the power of Satan to God, ᶜthat they may receive forgiveness of sins and ᵈan inheritance among those who are ᵉsanctified¹ by faith in Me.'

Paul's Post-Conversion Life

19"Therefore, King Agrippa, I was not disobedient to the heavenly vision, 20but ªdeclared first to those in Damascus and in Jerusalem, and throughout all the region of Judea, and *then* to the Gentiles, that they should repent, turn to God, and do ᵇworks befitting *repentance. 21For these reasons the Jews seized me in the temple and tried to kill *me*. 22Therefore, having obtained help from God, to this day I stand, witnessing both to small and great, saying no

Center reference column

21 ªActs 25:11, 12
22 ªActs 9:15
23 ªActs 9:15
¹pageantry
24 ªActs 25:2, 3, 7 ᵇActs 21:36; 22:22
*See WW at Heb. 7:25.
25 ªActs 23:9, 29; 26:31 ᵇActs 25:11, 12
*See WW at John 1:5.

CHAPTER 26
2 ª[1 Pet. 3:14; 4:14] ᵇ[1 Pet. 3:15, 16] ᶜActs 21:28; 24:5, 6
5 ª[Acts 22:3; 23:6; 24:15, 21]; Phil. 3:5
*See WW at 2 Pet. 2:1.
6 ªActs 23:6 ᵇ[Gen. 3:15; 22:18; 26:4; 49:10]; Deut. 18:15; 2 Sam. 7:12; Ps. 132:11; Is. 4:2; 7:14; 9:6; 40:10; Jer. 23:5; 33:14–16; Ezek. 34:23; 37:24; Dan. 9:24]; Acts 13:32; Rom. 15:8; [Titus 2:13]
*See WW at John 18:31.
7 ªJames 1:1 ᵇLuke 2:37; 1 Thess. 3:10; 1 Tim. 5:5 ᶜPhil. 3:11
9 ªJohn 16:2; 1 Cor. 15:9; 1 Tim. 1:12, 13 ᵇActs 2:22; 10:38 ¹against
10 ªActs 8:1–3; 9:13; Gal. 1:13 ᵇActs 9:14
11 ªMatt. 10:17; Acts 22:19
12 ªActs 9:3–8; 22:6–11; 26:12–18
16 ªActs 22:15; Eph. 3:6–8
*See WW at Rev. 1:5.
17 ªActs 22:21 ¹rescue ²NU, M omit *now*
18 ªIs. 35:5; 42:7, 16; Luke 1:79; [John 8:12; 2 Cor. 4:4]; Eph. 1:18; 1 Thess. 5:5 ᵇ2 Cor. 6:14; Eph. 4:18; 5:8; [Col. 1:13]; 1 Pet. 2:9 ᶜLuke 1:77 ᵈEph. 1:11; Col. 1:12 ᵉActs 20:32 ¹set apart
20 ªActs 9:19, 20, 22; 11:26 ᵇMatt. 3:8; Luke 3:8
*See WW at Matt. 3:2.

26:6, 7 See note on 24:14.

26:12–18 This is the third account in Acts of Paul's conversion (see 9:1–19; 22:6–21). **Kick against the goads:** See note on 9:5.

26:16, 17 These promises are not included in the other conversion accounts. In v. 17 Jesus promises His personal protection to

Paul, and His promise is fulfilled. Acts ends with Paul unharmed by the Jews and preaching the gospel freely in Rome.

26:19 God guides through supernatural means (**the heavenly vision**), but all such special guidance must be grounded in the unchanging revelation of the Bible.

KINGDOM DYNAMICS

26:19 Being Obedient to the Heavenly Vision, PROPHETIC DREAMS AND VISIONS. Four visions surrounded Paul's conversion in Acts: Stephen's stoning (7:55, 58, 59), Paul's experience near Damascus (9:3), Paul's vision in prayer (9:11, 12), and Ananias's vision (9:10, 17). Each time, Paul testified that the Lord spoke to him in a vision. His defense against those who thought him to be a heretic was that he "was not disobedient to the heavenly vision" (26:19).

As Charles Spurgeon said, "We must take care that we do not neglect heavenly monitions through fear of being considered visionary; we must not be staggered even by the dread of being styled fanatical, or out of our minds. For to stifle a thought from God is no small sin."

Note further the place visions played in the apostle Paul's experience (7:56—8:1; 9:1–16; 13:2–4; 14:19; 16:9, 10; 18:9–11; 22:17, 18; 27:22–25; 2 Cor. 12:1–4; Gal. 1:11, 12; 2:2; Eph. 3:1–5). (Matt. 2:12/2 Pet. 2:1) J.W.R.

WORD WEALTH

26:22 witnessing, *martureō;* Strong's #3140: Giving evidence, attesting, confirming, confessing, bearing record, speaking well of, giving a good report, testifying, affirming that one has seen, heard, or experienced something. In the NT it is used particularly for presenting the gospel with evidence. The English word "martyr" comes from this word, suggesting that a witness is one willing to die for his testimony.

other things than those [a]which the prophets and [b]Moses said would come— 23[a]that the Christ would suffer, [b]that He would be the first to rise from the dead, and [c]would proclaim light to the *Jewish* people and to the Gentiles."

Agrippa Parries Paul's Challenge

24Now as he thus made his defense, Festus said with a loud voice, "Paul, [a]you are

---

22 [a]Luke 24:27; Acts 24:14; 28:23; Rom. 3:21 [b]John 5:46
23 [a]Luke 24:26 [b]1 Cor. 15:20, 23; Col. 1:18; Rev. 1:5 [c]Is. 42:6; 49:6; Luke 2:32; 2 Cor. 4:4
24 [a]2 Kin. 9:11; John 10:20; [1 Cor. 1:23; 2:13, 14; 4:10]

25 [l]out of my mind
26 [a]Acts 26:3
29 [a]1 Cor. 7:7
31 [a]Acts 23:9, 29; 25:25
32 [a]Acts 28:18 [b]Acts 25:11

CHAPTER 27
1 [a]Acts 25:12, 25
2 [a]Acts 19:29
3 [a]Acts 24:23; 28:16
6 [a]Acts 28:11

---

beside yourself! Much learning is driving you mad!"

25But he said, "I am not [l]mad, most noble Festus, but speak the words of truth and reason. 26For the king, before whom I also speak freely, [a]knows these things; for I am convinced that none of these things escapes his attention, since this thing was not done in a corner. 27King Agrippa, do you believe the prophets? I know that you do believe."

28Then Agrippa said to Paul, "You almost persuade me to become a Christian."

29And Paul said, [a]"I would to God that not only you, but also all who hear me today, might become both almost and altogether such as I am, except for these chains."

30When he had said these things, the king stood up, as well as the governor and Bernice and those who sat with them; 31and when they had gone aside, they talked among themselves, saying, [a]"This man is doing nothing deserving of death or chains."

32Then Agrippa said to Festus, "This man might have been set [a]free [b]if he had not appealed to Caesar."

The Voyage to Rome Begins

27 And when [a]it was decided that we should sail to Italy, they delivered Paul and some other prisoners to *one* named Julius, a centurion of the Augustan Regiment. 2So, entering a ship of Adramyttium, we put to sea, meaning to sail along the coasts of Asia. [a]Aristarchus, a Macedonian of Thessalonica, was with us. 3And the next *day* we landed at Sidon. And Julius [a]treated Paul kindly and gave *him* liberty to go to his friends and receive care. 4When we had put to sea from there, we sailed under *the shelter of* Cyprus, because the winds were contrary. 5And when we had sailed over the sea which is off Cilicia and Pamphylia, we came to Myra, *a city* of Lycia. 6There the centurion found [a]an Alexandrian ship sailing to Italy, and he put us on board.

26:20 Works befitting repentance indicates that a true relationship with God will result in a godly lifestyle. We are not saved by our good works, but salvation by grace will certainly change us.

26:22, 23 See note on 24:14.

26:24–26 See note on 22:23.

26:27, 28 Paul's challenge to **Agrippa,** who had a Jewish heritage, put the king in an embarrassing position. If he agreed with Paul he would lose credibility with Festus, who had just declared Paul to be mad (v. 24). Yet if he renounced **the prophets** he would lose favor with the Jews. Therefore, he attempted to escape his dilemma by responding to Paul with what most interpreters feel to be an insincere and cynical comment: "In a short time you think to make me a Christian!"

27:1 This is the beginning of Paul's fourth trip, which takes him to Rome (see map of Paul's fourth journey). Luke shows

a remarkably detailed understanding of ancient seamanship. **Augustan Regiment** was one of five Roman regiments stationed near the seaport city of Caesarea.

27:2 Adramyttium was a seaport of the Roman province of Asia (modern Turkey). The ship Paul boarded was based there. **We put to sea** indicates that Luke was accompanying Paul on his final journey.

27:4 Paul's ship sailed to the north of **Cyprus** to protect itself from strong southerly winds.

27:5 Myra is a city in southern Asia Minor (modern Turkey).

27:6 The **Alexandrian ship,** probably a grain ship (v. 38), had its registry in Alexandria, the Roman capital of Egypt. Egypt was the principal source of grain for Rome, and the grain fleet was the lifeblood of the empire.

⁷When we had sailed slowly many days, and arrived with difficulty off Cnidus, the wind not permitting us to proceed, we sailed under the shelter of ᵃCrete off Salmone. ⁸Passing it with difficulty, we came to a place called Fair Havens, near the city of Lasea.

Paul's Warning Ignored

⁹Now when much time had been spent, and sailing was now dangerous ᵃbecause ¹the Fast was already over, Paul advised them, ¹⁰saying, "Men, I perceive that this voyage will end with **disaster** and much loss, not only of the cargo and ship, but also our lives." ¹¹Nevertheless the centurion was more persuaded by the helmsman and the owner of the ship than by the things spoken by Paul. ¹²And because the harbor was not suitable to winter in, the majority advised to set sail from there also, if by any means

7 ᵃActs 2:11; 27:12, 21; Titus 1:5, 12
9 ᵃLev. 16:29–31; 23:27–29; Num. 29:7
ᶦThe Day of Atonement, late September or early October

13 *See WW at Rom. 8:28.

WORD WEALTH

27:10 disaster, *hubris;* Strong's #5196: Hurt, loss, injury arising from violence, damage caused by the elements, hardship, detriment, trouble, and danger. In 2 Corinthians 12:10, where Paul described the reproaches he endured for the Lord's sake, *hubris* denotes insolence, impudence, a haughty attitude, insult, injury, outrage, persecution, and affront. The word is definitely adversarial. (Cf. "hubristic" and "hybrid.")

they could reach Phoenix, a harbor of Crete opening toward the southwest and northwest, *and* winter *there.*

In the Tempest

¹³When the south wind blew softly, supposing that they had obtained *their* *desire, putting out to sea, they sailed close by Crete.

27:9 The Fast is a reference to the Day of Atonement in late September or early October. It was already past, which was a way of saying winter's dangerous sailing weather was about to begin. The dangerous period for sailing began in mid-September and lasted until early November. After that, all navigation on the open sea halted until winter was over.

ON TO ROME (PAUL'S FOURTH JOURNEY, ACTS 27:1—28:16)

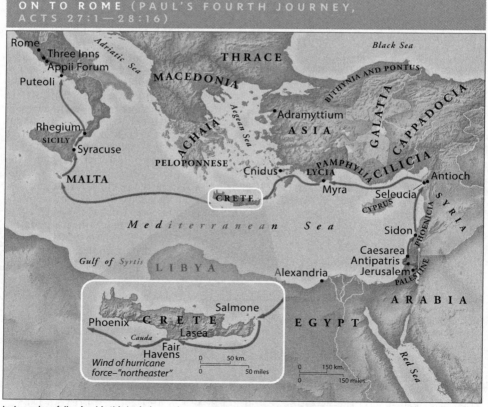

In Jerusalem following his third missionary journey, Paul struggled with Jews who accused him of profaning the temple (Acts 21:26–34). He was placed in Roman custody in Caesarea for two years, but after appealing to Caesar, was sent by ship to Rome. After departing the island of Crete, Paul's party was shipwrecked on Malta by a great storm. Three months later he finally arrived at the imperial city.

14But not long after, a tempestuous head wind arose, called [1]Euroclydon. 15So when the ship was caught, and could not head into the wind, we let *her* [1]drive. 16And running under *the shelter of* an island called [1]Clauda, we secured the skiff with difficulty. 17When they had taken it on board, they used cables to undergird the ship; and fearing lest they should run aground on the [1]Syrtis *Sands,* they struck sail and so were driven. 18And because we were exceedingly tempest-tossed, the next *day* they lightened the ship. 19On the third *day* [a]we threw the ship's tackle overboard with our own hands. 20Now when neither sun nor stars appeared for many days, and no small tempest beat on *us,* all hope that we would be saved was finally given up.

21But after long abstinence from food, then Paul stood in the midst of them and said, "Men, you should have listened to me, and not have sailed from Crete and incurred this *disaster and loss. 22And now I urge you to take [1]heart, for there will be no loss of life among you, but only of the ship. 23[a]For there stood by me this night an angel of the God to whom I belong and [b]whom I serve, 24saying, 'Do not be afraid, Paul; you must be brought before Caesar; and indeed God has *granted you all those who sail with you.' 25Therefore take heart, men, [a]for I believe God that it will be just as it was told me. 26However, [a]we must run aground on a certain island."

27Now when the fourteenth night had come, as we were driven up and down in the Adriatic *Sea,* about midnight the sailors sensed that they were drawing near some land. 28And they took soundings and found *it* to be twenty fathoms; and when they had gone a little farther, they took soundings again and found *it* to be fifteen fathoms. 29Then, fearing lest we should run aground on the rocks, they dropped four anchors from the stern, and [1]prayed for day to come. 30And as the sailors were seeking to escape from the ship, when they had let down the skiff into the sea, under pretense of putting out anchors from the prow, 31Paul said to the centurion and the soldiers, "Unless these men stay in the ship, you cannot be saved." 32Then the soldiers cut away the ropes of the skiff and let it fall off.

33And as day was about to dawn, Paul implored *them* all to take food, saying, "Today is the fourteenth day you have waited and continued without food, and eaten nothing. 34Therefore I urge you to take nourishment, for this is for your survival, [a]since not a hair will fall from the head of any of you." 35And when he had said these things, he took bread and [a]gave thanks to God in the presence of them all; and when he had broken *it* he began to eat. 36Then they were all encouraged, and also took food themselves. 37And in all we were two hundred and seventy-six [a]persons on the ship. 38So when they had eaten enough, they lightened the ship and threw out the wheat into the sea.

Shipwrecked on Malta

39When it was day, they did not recognize the land; but they observed a bay with a beach, onto which they planned to run the ship if possible. 40And they [1]let go the anchors and left *them* in the sea, meanwhile loosing the rudder ropes; and they hoisted the mainsail to the wind and made for shore. 41But striking [1]a place where two seas met, [a]they ran the ship aground; and the prow stuck fast and remained immovable, but the stern was being broken up by the violence of the waves.

42And the soldiers' plan was to kill the prisoners, lest any of them should swim away and escape. 43But the centurion, wanting to save Paul, kept them from *their* purpose, and commanded that those who could swim should jump *overboard* first and get to land, 44and the rest, some on boards and some on *parts* of the ship. And so it was [a]that they all escaped safely to land.

Paul's Ministry on Malta

28 Now when they had escaped, they then found out that [a]the island was called Malta. 2And the [a]natives[1] showed us unusual **kindness;** for they kindled a fire and made us all welcome, because of the rain that was falling and because of the cold. 3But when Paul had gathered a bundle of sticks and laid *them* on the fire, a viper came out because of the heat, and fastened on his hand. 4So when the natives saw the creature

---

14 [1]A southeast wind that stirs up broad waves; NU *Euraquilon,* a northeaster
15 [1]*be driven*
16 [1]NU *Cauda*
17 [1]M *Syrtes*
19 [a]Jon. 1:5
21 *See WW at Acts 27:10.
22 [1]*courage*
23 [a]Acts 18:9; 23:11; 2 Tim. 4:17 [b]Dan. 6:16; Rom. 1:9; 2 Tim. 1:3
24 *See WW at Col. 3:13.
25 [a]Luke 1:45; Rom. 4:20, 21; 2 Tim. 1:12
26 [a]Acts 28:1
29 [1]Or *wished*

34 [a]1 Kin. 1:52; [Matt. 10:30; Luke 12:7; 21:18]
35 [a]1 Sam. 9:13; Matt. 15:36; Mark 8:6; John 6:11; [1 Tim. 4:3, 4]
37 [a]Acts 2:41; 7:14; Rom. 13:1; 1 Pet. 3:20
40 [1]*cast off*
41 [a]2 Cor. 11:25 [1]A reef
44 [a]Acts 27:22, 31

CHAPTER 28
1 [a]Acts 27:26
2 [a]Acts 28:4; Rom. 1:14; 1 Cor. 14:11; Col. 3:11 [1]Lit. *barbarians*

27:16 The skiff was a smaller rowboat, or dinghy, used to transport people from a larger craft to the shore (see v. 30).

27:17 Cables were used to **undergird the ship** to prevent its breaking apart. **Syrtis:** Quicksands off the coast of North Africa.

27:18, 19 It was common for a ship's crew in a storm, in order to make the craft more buoyant, to throw virtually everything but the passengers overboard. They later disposed of their cargo

and remaining food (v. 38).

27:31, 32 Now everyone believed Paul (see vv. 10, 11, 21). The Roman **centurion** and his **soldiers** assumed command of this nonmilitary vessel.

27:38 See note on vv. 18, 19.

28:1 Malta is a small **island** just south of Sicily and Italy.

WORD ⚔ WEALTH

28:2 kindness, *philanthrōpia*; Strong's #5363: Compare "philanthropist" and "philanthropy." Love for mankind, hospitality, acts of kindness, readiness to help, human friendship, benevolence, and taking thought of others. The word is a compound of *philos*, "love," and *anthrōpos*, "man." In Titus 3:4, *philanthrōpia* is used to describe God's lovingkindness toward men.

hanging from his hand, they said to one another, "No doubt this man is a murderer, whom, though he has escaped the sea, yet justice does not allow to live." **5**But he shook off the creature into the fire and ᵃsuffered no harm. **6**However, they were expecting

5 ᵃMark 16:18; Luke 10:19

6 ᵃActs 12:22; 14:11
7 ˡMagistrate
8 ᵃActs 9:40; [James 5:14, 15] ᵇMatt. 9:18; Mark 5:23; 6:5; 7:32; 16:18; Luke 4:40; Acts 19:11, 12; [1 Cor. 12:9, 28]
*See WW at 2 Cor. 5:14.
9 *See WW at Matt. 12:22.
10 ᵃMatt. 15:6; 1 Tim. 5:17 ᵇ[Phil. 4:19]

that he would swell up or suddenly fall down dead. But after they had looked for a long time and saw no harm come to him, they changed their minds and ᵃsaid that he was a god.

7In that region there was an estate of the ˡleading citizen of the island, whose name was Publius, who received us and entertained us courteously for three days. **8**And it happened that the father of Publius lay *sick of a fever and dysentery. Paul went in to him and ᵃprayed, and ᵇhe laid his hands on him and healed him. **9**So when this was done, the rest of those on the island who had diseases also came and were *healed. **10**They also honored us in many ᵃways; and when we departed, they provided such things as were ᵇnecessary.

28:4 One of the pagan deities was a goddess called **justice.** The natives assumed she was behind this.

28:5 See note on Mark 16:17, 18.

28:7 Publius was the highest ranking Roman official on the island.

THE INFLUENCE OF PAUL

The witness of the apostle Paul began early in Damascus and in Tarsus, the city of his birth. Missionary travels then took him throughout the provinces of Galatia, Asia, Macedonia, and Achaia. Even while under custody in Caesarea and imprisoned in Rome, Paul testified of his salvation in Christ.

11 aActs 27:6
ʲGr. Dioskouroi,
Zeus's sons
Castor and
Pollux
14 aRom. 1:8
15 *See WW at
John 6:11.

| KINGDOM 🕊 DYNAMICS |

28:8, 9 Paul's Healing Ministry in Malta,
DIVINE HEALING. Here is a reference to divine healings in spite of the fact that Luke, a physician, accompanied Paul. This fact is so troublesome to critics of modern healing that some have come forth with the theory that the healings mentioned in v. 9 were the work of Luke who used medical remedies, although Luke is not mentioned by name. The theory is based on the use of *therapeuō*, the Greek word for "healing" (v. 8), which some insist refers to medical therapy.

In fact, however, this word occurs 34 times in the NT. In 32 instances it clearly refers to divine healing; in the other cases the use is general. Both words (*iaomai* and *therapeuō*) are used in reference to the same healing in Matthew 8:7, 8, indicating the terms are used interchangeably in the Bible.

This observation is certainly not to oppose medical treatment or to say medicine or medical aid is wrong. It is not. However, it does clarify that this text is not grounds for the substitution of medical therapy for prayer. God heals by many means: the prayer of faith, natural recuperative powers, medical aid or medicine, and miracles. (Acts 3:16/1 Cor. 12:9, 28) N.V.

Arrival at Rome

11After three months we sailed in aan Alexandrian ship whose figurehead was the ʲTwin Brothers, which had wintered at the island. 12And landing at Syracuse, we stayed three days. 13From there we circled round and reached Rhegium. And after one day the south wind blew; and the next day we came to Puteoli, 14where we found abrethren, and were invited to stay with them seven days. And so we went toward Rome. 15And from there, when the brethren heard about us, they came to meet us as far as Appii Forum and Three Inns. When Paul saw them, he *thanked God and took courage.

16Now when we came to Rome, the centurion delivered the prisoners to the captain of

16 aActs 23:11;
24:25; 27:3
17 aActs 23:29;
24:12, 13;
26:31 bActs
21:33
18 aActs 22:24;
24:10; 25:8;
26:32
19 aActs 25:11,
21, 25 ʲThe rul-
ing authorities
20 aActs 26:6, 7
bActs 26:29;
Eph. 3:1; 4:1;
6:20; 2 Tim.
1:8, 16; Philem.
10, 13
*See WW at
1 Thess. 1:3.
22 aLuke 2:34;
Acts 24:5, 14;
[1 Pet. 2:12;
3:16; 4:14, 16]
*See WW at
2 Pet. 2:1.
23 aLuke 24:27;
[Acts 17:3;
19:8] bActs
26:6, 22
24 aActs 14:4;
19:9
25 ʲNU your
*See WW at
Matt. 4:4.
26 aIs. 6:9, 10;
Jer. 5:21;
Ezek. 12:2;
Matt. 13:14,
15; Mark 4:12;
Luke 8:10;
John 12:40,
41; Rom. 11:8

the guard; but aPaul was permitted to dwell by himself with the soldier who guarded him.

Paul's Ministry at Rome

17And it came to pass after three days that Paul called the leaders of the Jews together. So when they had come together, he said to them: "Men *and* brethren, athough I have done nothing against our people or the customs of our fathers, yet bI was delivered as a prisoner from Jerusalem into the hands of the Romans, 18who, awhen they had examined me, wanted to let *me* go, because there was no cause for putting me to death. 19But when the ʲJews spoke against *it*, aI was compelled to appeal to Caesar, not that I had anything of which to accuse my nation. 20For this reason therefore I have called for you, to see *you* and speak with *you*, because afor the *hope of Israel I am bound with bthis chain."

21Then they said to him, "We neither received letters from Judea concerning you, nor have any of the brethren who came reported or spoken any evil of you. 22But we desire to hear from you what you think; for concerning this *sect, we know that ait is spoken against everywhere."

23So when they had appointed him a day, many came to him at *his* lodging, ato whom he explained and solemnly testified of the kingdom of God, persuading them concerning Jesus bfrom both the Law of Moses and the Prophets, from morning till evening. 24And asome were persuaded by the things which were spoken, and some disbelieved. 25So when they did not agree among themselves, they departed after Paul had said one *word: "The Holy Spirit spoke rightly through Isaiah the prophet to ʲour fathers, 26saying,

a'Go to this people and say:
"Hearing you will hear, and shall not
understand;
And seeing you will see, and not
perceive;

28:11 They had to wait **three months** until the sailing season began, probably in February. **The Twin Brothers** (see margin) were the patron deities of navigation.

28:12 **Syracuse** was the chief city on the island of Sicily.

28:13 **Puteoli,** modern Pozzuoli, was the principal port of southern Italy.

28:15 The party traveled overland to Rome on the Appian Way. **Appii Forum** was a town 43 miles from Rome, and **Three Inns** was located 33 miles from the capital city.

28:16 As a Roman citizen who had committed no flagrant offense and who had no political aspirations, Paul was allowed to live in private quarters.

28:20 **The hope of Israel** is the messianic kingdom in Jesus of Nazareth (see note on 24:14).

28:21 Paul had suffered intense persecution, and the Roman

Jews express a sense of surprise that his notoriety had not reached them.

28:22 These Roman Jews have not heard about Paul of Tarsus, but they have heard many negative reports about the Christian **sect.**

28:23 Basing his argument on the OT teachings concerning the Messiah and His **kingdom,** Paul presented the evidence pertaining to **Jesus.**

28:25–28 The closing message of Acts is that the Jews of Paul's day, from Jerusalem to Rome, rejected Jesus as their Messiah. Individual Jews believed, of course, but the torch of the gospel was passed from the Jewish nation to the Gentiles. Not only has Christianity spread from Jerusalem to Rome, it has also made the transition from an exclusively Jewish religion to a hope for all nations (v. 28). Paul himself thoroughly explains this transition in Rom. 9–11.

27 For the hearts of this people have
    grown dull.
  Their ears are hard of hearing,
  And their eyes they have closed,
  Lest they should see with *their* eyes
    and hear with *their* ears,
  Lest they should understand with *their*
    hearts and turn,
  So that I should heal them." '

28"Therefore let it be known to you that
the **salvation** of God has been sent ᵃto
the Gentiles, and they will hear it!" 29ʲAnd
when he had said these words, the Jews
departed and had a great dispute among
themselves.

30Then Paul dwelt two whole years in
his own rented house, and received all who
came to him, 31ᵃpreaching* the kingdom of
God and teaching the things which concern
the *Lord Jesus Christ with all *confidence,
no one forbidding him.

28 ᵃIs. 42:1, 6;
49:6; Matt.
21:41; Luke
2:32; Rom.
11:11
29 ʲNU omits
v. 29.

31 ᵃActs 4:31;
Eph. 6:19
*See WW at Acts
9:20. • See
WW at John
6:68. • See
WW at Acts
4:31.

WORD		WEALTH

28:28 salvation, *sōtērion;* Strong's #4992:
Rescue, deliverance, safety, liberation, release,
preservation, and the general word for Christian salvation. (Cf. "soteriology.") *Sōtērion*
only occurs five times. *Sōtēria,* the generic
word, occurs 45 times. It is an all-inclusive
word signifying forgiveness, healing, prosperity, deliverance, safety, rescue, liberation,
and restoration. Christ's salvation is total in
scope for the total man: spirit, soul, and body.

28:31 The term **kingdom of God** is not as prominent in Acts as it is in Luke's Gospel. Kingdom teachings, however, are the bookends of Acts. Jesus preached and demonstrated the kingdom; the apostles preached and demonstrated the kingdom in Acts, and Acts portrays Paul as continuing to preach the kingdom. For an account of Paul's probable activities following the completion of Acts, see Introduction to 1 Timothy: Author; also see Kingdom Dynamics articles on the kingdom of God.

TRUTH IN ACTION

THROUGH ACTS

Letting the Holy Spirit Bring God's Truth to Life in You

TRUTH		ACTION
ACTS TEACHES	**TEXT**	**ACTS INVITES**
(1) **Growing in Godliness** Conversion to faith in Jesus Christ is the first step to growing in godliness. Many such conversions are recorded in Acts. Here in detail is the message of the apostles and the response of the people. Here, also, is found the promise of the gift of the Holy Spirit to all who believe, an experience of empowering that was normative in the early church. Our message today remains the same regarding the gift of the Holy Spirit and the life He produces.	2:38–41	**Repent, be baptized,** and **receive** the gift of the Holy Spirit.
	3:19, 20	**Receive** complete forgiveness of your sins. **Enjoy** the refreshing that comes from God's presence.
	4:12	**Know** that only the name of Jesus Christ provides salvation.
	10:47, 48	**Remember** that water baptism was an integral part of the preaching of the apostles. **Affirm** and **uphold** this practice today.
(2) **Cultivating Dynamic Devotion** In the Old Testament only those uniquely called or anointed of God received the Holy Spirit. But under the New Covenant every believer is given the "Promise of the Father" (Luke 24:49), the active, indwelling presence of the Holy Spirit. By this activity of the Spirit's fullness in the life of every believer, dynamic devotion is possible and the ministry of Christ in His church continues.	1:8	**Believe** that the power of God comes only by the Holy Spirit. **Minister** in the power of the Holy Spirit.
	2:4; 4:8; 13:9	**Seek** and **receive** the baptism in the Holy Spirit. Continually be refilled with the Spirit to regularly renew your life and ministry. **Exercise** your prayer language as a part of the Spirit's ministry in your life.
	4:13	**Expect** your Spirit-filled relationship with Jesus to help you speak boldly, with courage and spiritual understanding.
	10:44, 45	**Share** Jesus boldly. **Ask** the Holy Spirit to confirm your testimony.

TRUTH		ACTION
ACTS TEACHES	**TEXT**	**ACTS INVITES**
③ **Lessons for Leaders** Acts contains indispensable material for those who wish to learn the power principles of Christian leadership. The leadership of the apostles in Acts is some of the most spiritually powerful the church has ever known. The leadership models here provide patterns for effective ministry and service. Applying the lessons for leaders given in Acts will help give today's Christian leader increased power in ministry.	2:42–47	Leaders, **incorporate** these four elements into your congregation's life: teaching, fellowship, breaking of bread, and prayers.
	6:1–6	Leaders, **allow** others to share in the work of the ministry.
	12:5	Leaders, **give** prayer a central place in your church life.
	13:1–3	Leaders, **submit** to the Spirit's guidance when confronting decisions. **Call** leadership to prayer and fasting in such times. **Release** freely those appointed and called by the Holy Spirit.
	14:14–18	Leaders, **remain** humble before the Lord and those you serve, giving Him all praise and honor.
	16:1–5	Leaders, **personally train** young people who are called to ministry.
	20:28–32	Leaders, **shepherd** God's beloved people of whom He has given you oversight. **Diligently guard** and **care** for the flock God has entrusted to you.
④ **The Walk of Faith** Acts summons us to a bold faith. The lives of the men and women in Acts challenge us to believe in our great God to do great things in great ways. These accounts invite us to the kinds of risks associated with this bold faith and inspire us to have the courage to follow these great examples.	3:21	**Believe steadfastly** that God will fulfill everything He has promised in His Word.
	14:3	**Humbly call** to the Lord to perform signs, wonders, and miracles to confirm with power the gospel message of His Son.